アメリカ人が語る日本の歴史
日本に迫る統一朝鮮(コリア)の悪夢

マックス・フォン・シュラー

AN AMERICAN SREAKS ON JAPANESE HISTORY
THE COMING JAPANESE NIGHTMARE, A UNIFIED KOREA

MAX VON SCHULER

アメリカ人が語る日本の歴史
日本に迫る統一朝鮮(コリア)の悪夢

An American speaks on Japanese history

The coming Japanese nightmare, a unified Korea

Introduction
はじめに

All these years I have lived in Japan, I have constantly been involved in debate about Article number 9, the anti-military clause of the Japanese constitution.

私はもうずいぶん長い間、日本に住んでいますが、これまで何度も憲法9条についての議論をしてきました。

In this book I will demonstrate how the existence of a military does not cause war, rather it prevents war. Peace is achieved through military strength. Countries do not attack countries with strong militaries, as it would be suicide.

本書では、軍隊の存在が戦争を引き起こすのではなく、逆に戦争を抑止するものであるということを論証しています。平和は軍事力によって保たれます。強力な軍隊を持つ国は攻撃されません。なぜなら、攻撃する側にとって、自殺行為になるからです。

I will also show how the Japanese people are not an aggressive race. I describe a war that could have been, but did not happen. That is the war between the Tokugawa Shogunate and Imperial Spain. Unlike Western countries, the Tokugawa Shogunate chose to isolate Japan from the fighting that Western countries brought to Asia.

さらに本書では、日本人は好戦的な民族ではないということを示しています。確かに徳川幕府とスペイン帝国の間で戦争が起きる可能性はありましたが、実際には起きませんでした。徳川幕府は、西洋諸国がやったようなアジア侵略には関わらず、鎖国を選びました。

Introduction

The difference in WWII was that the Tokugawa Shogunate had the military power to maintain it's existence. Imperial Spain could not possibly defeat the Tokugawa Shogunate. In WWII, a nation's existence depended upon access to resources, so to exist, Japan needed to expand.

大東亜戦争当時の日本と違い、徳川幕府は十分に国を守れる軍事力を持っていました。ですから、スペイン帝国が徳川幕府と戦って勝つことは不可能でした。一方、大東亜戦争の時は、国家が生存するには資源が必要であり、日本が存続するためには、世界に向かって勢力を拡大する必要がありました。

I will also write about how life would be in Japan if Japan had simply submitted to America. There are prominent Japanese who say that submission is the best course in case of a conflict. I will show how this would hell on earth for Japan.

あの当時、もし日本がおとなしく米国に服従していたら、日本はどうなっていたでしょうか。日本の著名人の中には、戦争になったらすぐに降伏すればいい、と言う人たちがいます。しかし、そういう選択をした場合、日本は地獄と化すであろうということを私は本書で説明します。

In addition I have written a simulation of the next most probable war for Japan. This would be with a newly unified North and South Korea, and since the South Korean Left is in such a hurry to unify, a United Korean conflict on Japan could happen in only a few years.

さらに、近い将来起きる可能性の高い、日本に対する武力攻撃についても、本書のChapter 9に書いています。これは、統一された北朝鮮と韓国が日本を攻撃するという戦争シミュレーションです。実際、韓国の左派は統一工作を急いでおり、数年以内に戦争が起きる可能性があります。

はじめに

I will describe how such war would go, without American help.

米軍の協力が得られない場合、この戦争はどのような様相を示すのでしょうか。そうしたことについて説明します。

I wrote this simulation in the summer of 2018, as what would happen if a unified Korea invaded Japan. In March of 2019, I do not see an immediate threat of this happening. However, events are proceeding rapidly inside South Korea, towards a quick reunification. Thusly, thinking about what would events would be likely in a quick reunification, my simulation could provide a good reference.

なお、本書で私が示した「統一コリアによる日本侵略のシミュレーション」は、2018年夏の時点で想定された一つの可能性であり、2019年3月の時点で全くその通りのことが起きているわけではありません。しかしその後も、統一コリア誕生の可能性はむしろ高まってきており、そうした統一コリア誕生後に何が起きるかを考える上で、私のシミュレーションは大いに参考になるでしょう。

Japan needs a military, it is time to cease such useless debate over the issue of a militarized Japan.

日本には軍隊が必要です。もう、国内で無駄な論争をするのは、やめるべき時がきているのです。

マックス・フォン・シュラー

Contents
もくじ

Introduction
はじめに / 3

Chapter 1　Japanese naivete about the world, and the reality of war
日本人は世界や戦争の現実について知らなさすぎる / 11

　The need for a Japanese military
　日本における軍隊の必要性……………………………………11

Chapter 2　Japanese are a non-aggressive race
日本人は好戦的な国民ではない / 14

　Americans know nothing about Japan
　日本のことを知らない米国人たち……………………………14

　The propaganda that Japanese are brutal
　「日本人は残虐」というプロパガンダ………………………18

　American Leftists want to turn Japan into their version of Utopia
　日本にユートピアを作ろうとした左派米国人………………23

Chapter 3　Why do wars happen?
なぜ戦争は起きるのか？ / 27

　Wars start because someone desires it
　戦争はいつも誰かの欲望から始まる…………………………27

　The Russians were deceived by America
　まんまと騙されたロシア人……………………………………30

もくじ

Chapter 4　America desired war with Great Britain just before WWII
第二次大戦の直前、米国は英国と戦争しようとしていた／34

America and Great Britain were not always friendly
米英は友好国などではなかった…………………………34

Chapter 5　Why was Japan not colonized?
なぜ日本は植民地にならなかったのか？／39

The coming of Perry to Japan and the American Civil war
ペリー来航と南北戦争……………………………………39

Chapter 6　The war that did not happen, the Tokugawa Shogunate attacks, defeats the Spanish Empire, annexes the Philippines
実現しなかった戦争、徳川幕府がスペインに勝利し、フィリピンを併合／43

A simulation of a war between Tokugawa Japan and Spain
日本vsスペインというシミュレーション………………43

The use of missionaries as an excuse for invasion
宣教師を利用した侵略……………………………………50

Americans only think of themselves
米国人は自分たちのことしか考えていない……………55

The first Sino-Japanese war and the Russo-Japanese war that surprised the world
世界を驚かせた日清日露戦争……………………………59

Chapter 7　What life would have been like if Japan had been colonized
日本が植民地になっていたら、どうなっていたか／63

Looking at the colonial policy of Imperial Briton
英国のインド支配に見る植民地政策……………………63

The greed of Western capitalists
強欲な西洋の資本家たち…………………………………66

The Japanese military fought bravely
日本軍は勇敢に戦った……………………………………68

Contents

The cruelty of war
戦争とは残酷なもの……………………………73

Colonialism, crueler than war
戦争よりもさらに残酷な占領……………………75

Present day America is heading for Civil war
内戦が近づいている米国………………………79

Foreigners lie very easily
平気で嘘をつく外国人…………………………80

For Americans, court cases are a form of cultural war
米国人にとって裁判は文化的な戦争である……………85

Chapter 8　Feminists destroy the US military's combat capability
フェミニストが米軍を弱体化させている／90

Feminists are destroying America
フェミニストが米国を崩壊させる…………………90

The idealism and reality of female troops
女性兵士の理想と現実…………………………92

The excessive promotion of minorities
過度にマイノリティを持ち上げる社会………………99

Difficulties with women in the military
女性が軍隊に入ることの問題点……………………104

How political correctness is weakening the military
軍隊を弱体化させるポリティカル・コレクトネス……108

Transgenderism and the military
軍隊とトランスジェンダー………………………112

Feminists will be the cause of future combat deaths
フェミニストが軍人たちの命を奪う………………113

Chapter 9　A simulation of war between Japan and a newly reunified Korea
日本と統一コリアの戦争シミュレーション／120

The day a unified Korea attacks Japan
統一コリアが日本に攻めてくる日…………………120

もくじ

An American female anti Japan President
米国に誕生する反日の女性大統領…………………124

The reality of unified Korea, and the wave of refugees
統一コリアの実態と押し寄せるコリア難民…………127

The intensification of anti Japanese activity in unified Korea
激化する統一コリアの反日活動……………………132

Unified Korea invades Fukuoka
統一コリアによる福岡上陸作戦……………………135

The nullification of the Japanese/American alliance, the rise of Japanese patriotism
日米同盟の無効化と日本人の蜂起…………………138

American troops in Japan revolt against orders not to fight
在日米軍兵士たちの反乱……………………………142

The creation of a Free Korea army in exile, and the end of the war
亡命革命軍の創設と戦争の終結……………………147

Chapter 10 An explanation of the simulation of war between Japan and a newly reunified Korea
日本と統一コリアの戦争シミュレーションについての解説／ 151

We should learn from the tragedy of history
歴史の悲劇に学べ……………………………………151

The Deep State that actually rules America
米国を裏で操るディープ・ステート………………153

Identity politics and Feminists
アイデンティティ政治とフェミニスト……………155

South Koreans do not know history or reality
歴史の真実を知らない韓国人………………………160

The Kim family and the power brokers of North Korea
金一族と北朝鮮の権力者たち………………………162

The lies and exaggerations of the anti Japan movement
嘘と誇張の反日活動…………………………………165

The Korean war and the escapees from the North
朝鮮戦争と脱北者……………………………………168

Contents

Could the internet destroy North Korea?
インターネットが北朝鮮を滅ぼす？……………………171

Moon Jae In, the most dangerous President
文在寅という最も危険な大統領……………………175

Who are Korean residents of Japan?
在日コリアンという存在………………………………179

The nature of the fighting in Fukuoka city
福岡市付近での戦闘……………………………………181

The effects of Nodong missile attacks
ノドンミサイルによる攻撃……………………………183

Would the North Koreans use nuclear weapons?
北朝鮮は核兵器を使用するのか？……………………187

The fighting ability of the Self Defense forces and lessons of the First World war
自衛隊の実戦能力と第一次大戦の教訓…………………189

The possibility of American military revolt
米軍兵士による反乱の可能性…………………………196

The people of unified Korea would suffer the most
最も苦しむのは統一コリアの国民たち…………………199

North Korean commandos and the Gwangju incident
北朝鮮工作員による光州事件…………………………202

Unified Korea and China
統一コリアと中国………………………………………206

Who would benefit from war?
誰がこの戦争で得をするのか？………………………210

Afterward
おわりに／212

Chapter 1
Japanese naivete about the world, and the reality of war
日本人は世界や戦争の現実について知らなさすぎる

The need for a Japanese military
日本における軍隊の必要性

I have lived in Japan for 44 years. One quickly notices that so many Japanese people have no understanding of the need for a Japanese military. And many people doubt the capabilities of the present day Japanese military.

私は、日本に住んで44年が過ぎました(2018年現在)。日本に長く住んでいると、多くの日本人が軍隊の必要性を理解していないということがよく分かります。それと同時に彼らは、日本の軍隊である自衛隊の実力というものを、よく分かっていません。

Also, many people have an extremely benevolent view of America. There are people who believe that any social trend that starts in America should be adopted in Japan. Yet not all social trends in America are benign, and that is especially true today.

また、多くの日本人が非常に親米的であることも分かります。その中には、米国の社会的風潮を日本も取り入れた方がよいと信じている人もいます。しかし、そうした米国発のものが全ていいものとは限りません。特に最近の風潮はそうです。

I am beginning to write this book in August of 2018. August 15th is the

Chapter1 Japanese naivete about the world, and the reality of war

day Japan surrendered to the Allies in Word War II, and every August, the left-leaning Japanese media goes into a frenzy on how terrible Japan was in the war.

　私は 2018 年 8 月から本書を書き始めました。8 月 15 日は日本が連合軍に降伏した日です。毎年 8 月になると、左翼マスコミは熱心に、先の戦争で日本はいかにひどいことをしたか、という情報を垂れ流します。

It often spills over into discussions on how backward Japan still is today, compared to enlightened countries of the West. Frankly, it is sickening.

　さらにこの手の報道は、進んだ西洋諸国と比べると日本は今も遅れているという話に及ぶことが多く、それを聞くたびに、私はうんざりしています。

A live fire exercise exhibition at Mount Fuji.
陸上自衛隊による富士総合火力演習

第1章　日本人は世界や戦争の現実について知らなさすぎる

Well meaning but naive and ignorant Japanese people tell me that if Japan had an army, it would cause war. This seems to be a central pillar of left-wing Japanese thought in this day and age.

また、日本が軍隊を持つとまた戦争を起こしますよ、と私に話しかけてくる日本人がいます。現実が見えていない人たちです。これは、日本の左翼思想の中心的な考えのようです。

It is extremely insulting to the Japanese people. What the Left does not realize is it's true meaning. What is means is that Japanese people are by nature of birth defective, and if a military exists in Japan, then Japanese people will automatically riot out of control and destroy things.

実は、こうした発言は日本人を露骨に侮辱するものです。しかし左派の人たちは、その言葉が何を意味するのか、まるで分かっていません。つまりこれは、日本人は生まれつき知能に障害があり、武器を持たせたら勝手に暴走して何でもかんでも破壊してしまう、ということを言っているのと同じことだからです。

It means that Japanese people are subhuman. This was the thinking of the Americans who wrote the Japanese Constitution.

これは、「日本人は人間以下の存在である」と言っているのと同じであり、今の日本国憲法を書いた米国人はそのように考えていた、ということでもあるのです。

Chapter 2
Japanese are a non-aggressive race
日本人は好戦的な国民ではない

Americans know nothing about Japan
日本のことを知らない米国人たち

Let me ask a question of you, my readers. What country had a military government, with a large standing army, for a great period of time without engaging in war?

読者の方々に質問があります。大規模な兵力を有した軍事政権の国で、最も長いあいだ戦争をしなかったのはどこだと思いますか？

Well that is Japan. The Tokugawa Shogunate. For 263 years, The Tokugawa Shogunate existed as a military government, with a large standing army. Yet they did not invade any other country.

答えは日本の徳川幕府です。軍事政権である徳川幕府は263年もの長きにわたって存続し、その間、大規模な兵力を有していました。しかし、他国を侵略することはありませんでした。

Toyotomi Hideyoshi, with his two invasions of Korea, was an exception. Japanese people are simply not an aggressive people.

豊臣秀吉は二度朝鮮に侵攻しましたが、これは例外です。日本人は好戦的な民族ではありません。

So why The Great Pacific War? It is very simple: the existence of aggressive Western powers creating colonies in Asia. Japan moved to protect it's own existence.

では、なぜ大東亜戦争が起こったのでしょうか？　答えは簡単です。好戦的な西洋列強が、アジアに植民地を築いていたからです。日本は自衛のために戦ったのです。

I am not sure how these left-wing people think that Japan can continue to exist without a military. They seem to have some hazy idea that somehow there will be world peace.

先ほど登場したような左派の人たちが、軍隊なしでどうやって日本という国が存続できると考えているのか、私にはよく分かりません。おそらく彼らは、ただ何となく、世界は平和になるんだろうという、漠然としたイメージを持っているだけなのでしょう。

It is not only naive, but dangerous. Japanese people have never been subjugated, never been enslaved. Frankly, in the post-World War II American occupation of Japan, we were very lucky that certain Americans led it.

これは、彼らがただ単におめでたいというだけではなく、非常に危険な考えなのです。日本人は一度も他民族に支配されたことがありませんし、奴隷にされたこともありません。大東亜戦争で敗れ、日本は占領されましたが、その占領が米国主導によるものだったことは、日本にとってとても幸運なことでした（占領を主導したのは特定の米国人です）。

There were many other Americans who wanted to seriously punish Japan, or to destroy the Japanese economy so that Japan would never become a powerful country again. They felt that the concept of a powerful non-White, non-Christian country to be insulting.

当時、多くの米国人が日本を厳罰に処すべきだと考えていました。

Chapter2 Japanese are a non-aggressive race

二度と再び、日本が強い国になれないよう、日本の経済を破壊すべきだと考えていたのです。彼らにとって、非白人の非キリスト教国が自分たちの脅威となることは、許しがたいことでした。

The American occupation Authorities were mostly Leftists; people who had participated in the New Deal of President Roosevelt. And like Leftists everywhere, they dreamed of creating a new world, a new time of human beings -- a new Utopia.

占領軍の局員はほとんどが左派に属し、ルーズベルト大統領のニューディール政策に参画した人たちでした。そして、ほとんどの左派の人たちと同じように、新しい世界、新しい時代、新しいユートピアを創ることを夢見ていました。

During the war, the American government had prepared thousands of specialists in Japan, trained in the Japanese language, Japanese culture and history. Not one of them was used in Japan in the occupation headquarters. In fact only a few made it to Japan only to be assigned to Okinawa or remote prefectures in Japan. None of the Japanese-trained specialists had any effect on Occupation policy.

戦時中、米国政府は、戦後の占領政策のために、日本語、日本文化、そして日本の歴史を学んだ何千人もの日本の専門家を用意しました。しかしGHQ内部では、これらの専門家を用いることはせず、ごく一部の専門家が沖縄などに割り当てられただけでした。つまり、彼ら日本の専門家は占領政策に何の影響も及ぼしませんでした。

This kind of thinking is common among Americans. They do not trust other Americans who speak multiple languages, or understands the culture of another country. They prefer the type of person who believes America is the best culture in the world, and who tries to force others to become like Americans.

第2章　日本人は好戦的な国民ではない

米国人は一般的に、他国の言葉や文化を理解している米国人を信用しません。彼らは米国が世界で最も優れた文化を持つ国であると信じており、他国に"米国"を強制しようとします。

And this is why America constantly makes mistakes internationally in war and diplomacy. And Americans never learn from these mistakes.

これこそが、米国が外交や戦争で、国際的に絶えず間違いを犯す理由です。そして、米国人は何度こうした間違いを犯しても、そこから学ぶことはありません。

So these idealistic left-wing Americans were free to create the society they wanted to make. They created the myth of the evil Japanese leadership, who exploited the Japanese population. This myth was also presented to the American people.

それで、こうした理想主義的な左派の米国人が日本に、自分たちが望む社会を勝手に造りました。彼らは、邪悪な日本の指導者が日本国民を不当に搾取していたという神話を作り、この神話は、米国民にも教え込まれました。

Colonel Kades himself, who had such an effect upon Japan, admitted that he had had no knowledge about Japan at all before arriving.

占領下の日本に大きな影響を与えたケーディス大佐は、日本に来るまで日本のことをよく知らなかったということを認めています。

Colonel Kades,
assistant chief of government section, GHQ.

GHQ民政局次長
チャールズ・L・ケーディス大佐

17

Chapter2 Japanese are a non-aggressive race

The propaganda that Japanese are brutal
「日本人は残虐」というプロパガンダ

　For years during the war, American wartime propaganda had depicted Japanese people as a vicious and subhuman race. The American response to this was extermination. Thus, no American made any protest about the strategic bombing of Japan, which was not military in nature but was indeed genocide.

　戦時中、米国は、日本人を狂暴で劣った人種のように宣伝しました。それを真に受けた米国人は、日本人を皆殺しにしろ、と叫びました。日本に対する戦略爆撃（事実上の大虐殺）に抗議する米国人は、ほとんどいませんでした。

The Asakusa district has become a burnt out field.

焼け野原となった浅草

第2章　日本人は好戦的な国民ではない

There is no other thing to call it. When you deliberately target civilians in a conflict, you wish to end their race. Well this type of warfare is common among Caucasians. In a previous book, I have used the example of Japanese castles to illustrate this.

実際、あれは虐殺以外の何物でもありません。意図的に民間人を攻撃目標にしたのは、その民族を絶滅させてやる、という意志があるからです。まあ、白人の間ではよくあることですが。私は以前の著書で、日本のお城を例にして、このことを説明しました。

Japanese castles protected the Feudal Lord, his retainers, and their families. The towns and cities of Japan had no fortifications whatsoever. All of Japan's wars, fought by the famed Samurai, were between Feudal Lords. The townspeople were not involved.

日本のお城は、大名や家臣、その家族を守るものでした。日本の街は、城郭で守られていません。かつての日本の戦争はほとんど全て、大名、武士の間で戦われました。つまり、街の人たちは戦いに関係ありませんでした。

In other countries however, wars are affairs of extermination of one race over another. Japan has had no experience of this. And this is the reason so many Japanese people have accepted American propaganda about The Great Pacific War.

しかし、他の国では、戦争とは、ある民族が他の民族を絶滅させるということです。そして日本には、そのような戦争の経験がありませんでした。米国のプロパガンダがすんなり日本に浸透したのは、米国もそのようなことをやる国だということを、多くの日本人が知らなかったからです。

When I see Japanese people, Leftists saying things like, "the Japanese Imperial Army is responsible for all the civilians who died on Okinawa."

Chapter2 Japanese are a non-aggressive race

Or, "The Emperor is responsible for the American bombings of Japanese cities", and I feel a great sadness in my heart.

　日本人の左派の人々が、例えば、「沖縄で民間人が大勢亡くなった責任は日本軍にある」「日本への本土空襲は天皇に責任がある」などと言っているのを聞くと、私はとても悲しくなります。

The Japanese military had no control over where America would attack. The three choices at the end of the war were Okinawa, Taiwan, or the Philippines.

　当時の米軍は、どこでも自由に攻撃することができました。大戦末期、攻撃の候補は3カ所ありました。沖縄、台湾、フィリピンです。

There are many stories being said by Japanese Leftists that the Imperial Army forced Japanese civilians to kill themselves in Okinawa. Well, terrible things happen in war. But the truth is, American troops do not actually have a good record. They rob, rape and kill civilians. They was very true in WWII. I am not singling out Americans here, this is normal conduct in wartime. For any country.

　日本の左派の人たちはよく、日本軍は沖縄で民間人に自決を強要した、と言います。確かに、戦争では恐ろしいことが起こります。実際、米国兵はろくなことをしていません。民間人の殺害、レイプ、強盗などです。第二次世界大戦では、よくありました。ただこれは米国人に限った話ではなく、戦争ではよく見られる行為でした。

Except Japan. Japanese troops had generally good behavior towards civilians. If you search the net, you can find many stories of American troops' nastiness.

　しかし、日本は違います。民間人に対して、日本軍は一般的に品行方正でした。ネットで検索すれば、米国兵の悪行が大量に出てきます。

第2章　日本人は好戦的な国民ではない

Japanese troops in WWII had a code of honor, the code of the warrior. To kill or harm civilians was dishonorable. It sometimes did happen, but in general it did not. Americans however did not have a code of honor until after the Korean war. And that only refers to not betraying the United States if taken prisoner.

大東亜戦争下の日本兵には、具体的な行動規範である戦陣訓がありました。そこでは、民間人の殺害は不名誉なことでした。全くなかったわけではありませんが、ほとんどの日本兵がそのようなことを行わなかったのです。一方の米国兵は、朝鮮戦争後まで行動規範がなく、あったのは、捕虜になっても米国を裏切ってはならない、という規範だけでした。

American GI playing with a Japanese skull.

日本兵の頭蓋骨をおもちゃにする米国兵

Chapter2 Japanese are a non-aggressive race

Rape by American troops was pervasive during the battle of Okinawa, and after. In Occupation Japan, a maternity hospital was entered by a gang of US troops who threw the infants on the floor to die, and raped the female patients. In Nagoya in 1946 US troops cut the phone lines of a city block, entered the houses, and raped all the women they could find. Rapes numbered over 300 per day.

沖縄戦、そして戦後も、米国兵によるレイプ事件は頻発していました。占領期間中、ある産科病院に米国兵の集団が侵入し、赤ちゃんを床に投げつけて殺害、入院女性たちを次々レイプしたこともありました。1946年、名古屋市では街の一角の電話線を切断して家々に侵入し、女性を見つけ次第レイプしました。レイプ事件は毎日300件以上、起きていました。

Japanese troops play with Chinese children after the fall of Nanking.

陥落後の南京で中国人の子供と玩具で遊ぶ日本兵

American troops were not at all well behaved like Western commentators assert. And troublesome American behavior with women continues to this day.

欧州の評論家たちが罵ったように、米国兵の行動は品行方正からは程遠いものでした。しかも米国兵の女性に対する問題行動は、今も続いています。

So it was in the interest of Americans after the war to create propaganda that the Japanese Imperial Army and Navy were evil, and they did so. And for the most part, the Japanese populace has believed this.

これらを覆い隠すために、戦後米国人は、日本軍が悪魔のような存在であったというプロパガンダを流しました。そして日本人の多くも、それを信じています。

They have forgotten the sacrifices made by the Japanese Imperial Armed Forces to keep Japan and Asia free.

日本人は、日本軍が日本を守り、アジアを解放するために、多大な犠牲を払ったことを忘れています。

American Leftists want to turn Japan into their version of Utopia
日本にユートピアを作ろうとした左派米国人

So these idealistic left-wing Americans of the Occupation, in their zeal to create some kind of Utopia, bestowed Article Number 9 of the Japanese Constitution upon us, and are responsible for immense problems today.

さて、この占領時代の理想主義的な左派米国人は、彼らにとってのユートピアを創ろうという熱意から、日本国憲法に第9条を設けました。つまり彼らには、現在起きている数多くの問題に対して責任があるのです。

Chapter2 Japanese are a non-aggressive race

There is something I must explain about left-wing Americans. It is easy to identify the greed of American capitalists and corporate presidents. They wish to destroy every competing company, and take all possible wealth for their own.

左派米国人の性格について、一つ説明しなければならないことがあります。例えば、米国の資本主義者、企業の社長の強欲さは、皆さんも理解しやすいことでしょう。彼らは競合他社が不利益をこうむるようなことをしてでも、できるだけ自分たちの富を増やそうと考えます。

But what of the Leftist person? They claim to be motivated by social justice. However, in their own way, they are just as greedy. Instead of gaining control over an entire market, they deal in ideas.

それでは、左派はどうでしょうか？　彼ら自身は、社会的公正の実現のために行動していると主張しています。しかし結局、彼らのやり方も、前者と同じように強欲です。彼らは市場を独占するのではなく、理念を独占しようとするのです。

To the Leftist, any other social idea must be totally destroyed and eradicated. That is why left-wing revolutions are always so bloody. They cannot tolerate the existence of people who think differently, so they kill them.

左派の人たちにとって、自分たち以外の社会的理念は、徹底的に打ちのめし、根絶する必要があります。ですので、左派の革命は常に流血の惨事となります。彼らは、異なる考えの人間の存在を容認できないので、その人たちを文字通り抹殺するのです。

When the American occupation came to Japan, they dispensed with experts who had knowledge about the country, and looked at Japan as a place to carry out their social fantasies.

第2章 日本人は好戦的な国民ではない

　前述したように、米国が日本を占領した時、彼らは日本についての専門家を用いませんでした。その上で彼らは、自分たちの社会的空想を日本で実行しようと考えました。

Today's Japanese Leftists, not understanding this, attempt to continue this work of destroying Japanese society.

　今の日本の左派は、そういう事実を理解せず、それを引き継いで日本社会を破壊する作業を続けています。

The truth is, when Americans foisted this concept that the Imperial Army and Navy were the cause of war upon Japan, they had no understanding of Japanese people or culture. Instead, they were really referring to themselves.

　米国人は日本人に、日本軍が戦争の惨禍をもたらしたのだいう考えを押しつけましたが、彼らは日本人や日本の文化のことを理解しておらず、米国自身がやったことを日本がやったように言っていただけです。

Since they did not understand Japanese people, or any other nation, they could only use themselves as a model. Perhaps they well remembered the 1930's rainbow war plans, Red for Great Britain, Green for Mexico, Black for Germany, Orange for Japan, Citron for Brazil, Emerald for Ireland, Indigo for Iceland, Lemon for Portugal, and White for domestic revolution. There are many more plans for other nations. They are called the "Rainbow war plans".

　彼らは、日本人や他の国のことをよく知らないので、モデルとして自分自身を使うしかありません。おそらく彼らは、1930年代の戦争計画を思い出したのでしょう。赤は英国、緑はメキシコ、黒はドイツ、オレンジは日本、シトロンはブラジル、エメラルドはアイルランド、インディゴはアイスランド、レモンはポルトガル、白は

Chapter2 Japanese are a non-aggressive race

米国での内戦です。それ以外の国にも色を割り当てて計画が立てられ、それらは「レインボー戦争計画」と呼ばれています。

Since Americans are so warlike, they assumed that Japanese people must be the same. So to their thinking, if Japan did not have a military, Japan would become docile and dependent upon America.

米国人はとても好戦的ですから、日本人も同じにちがいないと考えました。それで、占領政策で日本が軍隊を持てないようにすれば、従順になり、米国に依存する国になると考えたわけです。

One more thing. The Americans who wrote the Japanese Constitution thought that Japan would always be a vassal state of America. Vassal states are always plundered by the dominant country. They never imagined that in few short years with the Korean war, America would need Japan as a military ally, and that Article 9 of the Constitution would be a major impediment.

もう一つ。日本国憲法を書いた米国人たちは、日本は以後永遠に米国の属国になると考えていました。属国は常に支配国から収奪されます。彼らは、その後の朝鮮戦争で日本が米国の軍事同盟国として必要になることや、憲法第9条が大きな障害になることを、全く想像していませんでした。

Chapter 3
Why do wars happen?
なぜ戦争は起きるのか？

Wars start because someone desires it
戦争はいつも誰かの欲望から始まる

It is not because an Army exists in a certain country. As a former Marine, I can tell you that the military trains you to seek out weakness in an opponent. If an opponent is too strong, no one will attack.

「軍隊があるから戦争が起きる」のではありません。私は元米海兵隊員なので知っていますが、軍の訓練では敵の弱点を探すことを教えます。敵が強過ぎるのであれば、誰も攻撃しません。

Wars arise out of greed. Sometimes it is just to obtain more riches, sometimes it is a need for food, or resources. Wars happen due to racial or ethnic hatred.

戦争は欲望から始まります。もっと富を得ようとして始まることもあるし、食料や資源の必要性から始まることもあります。また戦争は、民族、人種間の憎悪が原因で始まることもあります。

So many Japanese believe America's propaganda that Japan was an evil nation in WWII. No. It was the other way around. If any one was awful, it was the administration of President Roosevelt. They knew Pearl Harbor was coming. The Japanese mobile strike force, the carrier fleet was tracked as it approached Hawaii.

Chapter3 Why do wars happen?

　多くの日本人は、日本が悪の国であったという米国のプロパガンダを信じています。でもそれは違います。逆です。ひどかったのはルーズベルト政権の方です。彼らは真珠湾が攻撃されることを知っていました。日本の機動部隊がハワイに接近するのを、米国は追跡していました。

The US troops on the island were deliberately sacrificed so that America would appear to be the victim of a surprise attack. At the time, the average American did not want war. But the Roosevelt administration did.

　米国が卑劣な騙し討ちを受けたことにするために、ハワイの米国兵は生け贄にされたのでした。当時、米国民は戦争を望んでいませんでした。しかし、ルーズベルト大統領は戦争を望んでいました。

Today Americans will say that America went to war to destroy the horrors of Nazi Germany, and to save the Jewish people. That is not true either.

　今の米国人は、米国が第二次世界大戦に参戦した理由は、ナチスドイツの恐怖からユダヤ人を救うためだったと言います。それも事実ではありません。

America went to war to achieve economic dominance over the entire globe. In Nazi Germany as of 1941, while the persecution of Jews was severe, the extermination of Jews as in the holocaust had not yet begun. Even after the holocaust began, America made no effort to stop it.

　米国の参戦理由は、世界規模の経済的支配を獲得するためでした。1941年のナチスドイツでは、ユダヤ人に対する迫害は深刻でしたが、ホロコーストはまだ始まっていませんでした。始まった後も、米国はホロコーストを阻止しようとはしませんでした。

But what could America have done to prevent this extermination? By 1943, when the extermination camps were being built, the Americans knew about them, and what they were. At this time, America had significant bomber forces in Europe. They could have bombed the camps, or at least the rail road yards that handled the trains bringing Jewish people to be killed.

では、米国はこの虐殺を阻止できたのでしょうか？ 1943年までに絶滅収容所の建設が始まっていましたが、米国政府はその建設中の収容所の存在や、その目的も知っていました。しかも当時、米軍はヨーロッパに大規模な爆撃戦力を展開していました。だから、その収容所や、虐殺されるユダヤ人を運ぶ列車の車両基地を爆撃することは可能でした。

It would not have ended the Holocaust, but it would have caused serious delays in the extermination of Jews, and the other peoples killed in the camps.

Birkenau Extermination Camp.

ビルケナウ絶滅収容所

Chapter3 Why do wars happen?

それを実行していれば、大量虐殺を完全には阻止できないまでも、大幅に遅らせることはできたでしょう。

And it would have sent a serious signal to the German Nazi government. Yet despite America having a very large Air Force in Europe, nothing like this was done. Instead, the Americans concentrated on bombing the industry of Germany and nations occupied by the German military.

そしてそれは、ナチスドイツに対して重要なシグナルになったはずです。しかし、米国はそれを実行しませんでした。ヨーロッパに大規模な航空部隊があったのに、米国はドイツの工業地帯や占領地ばかり空襲していました。

I think the true purpose of this bombing campaign was to insure that no European nation would arise as an industrial power after the war. In Japan, the bombing was done to exterminate the Japanese population.

しかも、この空襲の本当の目的は、戦後、ヨーロッパに工業大国が生まれないようにすることだったと思います。一方で、日本に対する空襲は、日本人を絶滅させるのが目的でした。

The Russians were deceived by America
まんまと騙されたロシア人

A little historical note. 80% of the trucks used by the Soviet military in WWII were supplied by America in the "lend-lease" program. Post war, the Soviet Union was in dire shape. The major industrial areas of the Western Soviet Union had seen severe fighting, and were devastated. The lend-lease agreement was that equipment provided to the Soviet Union would be returned once the war ended.

一つ、歴史の豆知識を紹介しましょう。第二次世界大戦でソ連軍

が使ったトラックの８割は、米国からレンドリース法（武器貸与法）に基づいて提供されたものでした。戦後、ソ連は大変な状態になりました。ソ連西部の主な工業地域は戦場となり、荒廃してしまったためです。レンドリース法では、ソ連に提供した装備は戦後、米国に返還することになっていました。

The Soviets asked to keep those trucks, as they were sturdy and tough, and would have been a great help after the war in rebuilding the Soviet Union. America replied "No". So the Soviets adhered to the agreement and returned the trucks.

しかし、頑丈な米国のトラックはソ連の再建にとても役立つので、ソ連政府は米国政府に対して、継続での使用を依頼しました。それに対する米国の返事は「ノー」です。それで、仕方なくソ連はその合意を守り、トラックを米国に返還しました。

America built a special ship, with a huge iron claw. It anchored in international waters 3 miles from shore, outside Murmansk.

すると米国は、大きな鉄の爪を持つ特殊な船を造りました。その船は、ソ連ムルマンスクの海岸から３マイルの公海に停泊しました。

Soviet Russia dutifully delivered those trucks to America at Murmansk. They were taken to the special ship with the claw. There, they were destroyed in full view of the Russian people. The claw would crush the chassis of the vehicle, so they could not be used.

ソ連は、律儀にムルマンスク港で米国にトラックを返還しました。米国はその大きな鉄の爪を持つ特殊な船にトラックを載せ、海岸のロシア人がよく見えるところで、そのトラックを潰しました。大きな鉄の爪でトラックのシャーシを押しつぶし、使い物にならないようにしたのです。

America really did not want the trucks back, and they did not need

Chapter3 Why do wars happen?

them. But they wanted to send a message to the Russians, it was "Die!" They did not want Russia to develop into a power that could compete with America.

　実際のところ、米国はトラックなど不要で、返してもらいたいなどとは思っておらず、ただ単にロシア人にメッセージを伝えたかったのです。「くたばれ！」というメッセージです。ソ連が戦後発展し、米国の競争相手になることを望んでいなかったのです。

When the Soviet Union collapsed in 1991, America used the government of Boris Yeltsin to attempt to turn Russia into an American vassal state. Vladimir Putin put a stop to this, and ensured Russian Independence. That is why the American Deep State hates Vladimir Putin so much today.

　1991年にソ連が崩壊した時、米国はエリツィン政権を利用して、ロシアを米国の属国にしようとしていました。しかしプーチン大統領がそれを阻止し、ロシアの独立を守りました。そういうわけで、現在の米国のディープ・ステート（権力の黒幕）はプーチンが大嫌いなのです。

The American WWII goal was total dominance of the planet. Back in WWII Japan, Japanese Prime Minister Prince Konoe offered to meet every American demand, including withdrawal of Japanese troops from northern China.

　米国にとって第二次世界大戦の最終目標は、全世界の支配でした。大戦前の日本の総理大臣だった近衛文麿は、陸軍の北支からの撤退を含む、米国の要求を全て呑むと申し出ました。

But America refused to negotiate with Japan. America launched an oil embargo that they knew would force Japan to attack America out of desperation. They knew that America could absorb a first strike by Japan and counter attack.

しかし、米国は日本との交渉を拒否しました。その上で、日本が米国を攻撃せざるを得なくなることが分かっていて、米国は対日石油禁輸を開始しました。日本に第一撃を撃たせれば、米国は日本を攻撃できるようになるからです。

That was correct. America was not interested in peace with Japan: it's goal was total destruction of Japan.

それは狙い通りでした。米国は日本との和平には関心がありませんでした。米国の目標は、日本を滅亡させることだったからです。

For those Japanese people who still believe American propaganda, Japan had no choice but to fight.

米国のプロパガンダをまだ信じている日本人のために言います。日本には、戦う以外の選択肢はなかったのです。

Chapter 4
America desired war with Great Britain just before WWII
第二次大戦の直前、米国は英国と戦争しようとしていた

America and Great Britain were not always friendly
米英は友好国などではなかった

Before WWII, the greatest world empire was the British Empire. America desired to destroy it. A war with the British Empire was very possible until just before WWII, when America decided Great Britain would be an ally.

第二次世界大戦前、世界最大の帝国は英国でした。米国は、この帝国を滅ぼしたいと思っていました。その後、第二次世界大戦が始まったため、米国は英国と組むことになりましたが、その直前まで、英国との戦争は十分に起こり得るものでした。

This was War Plan Red. It envisioned an invasion of Canada, along with amphibious landings in Halifax Canada. The British home islands were to be hit by bombing raids using chemical weapons. Islands in the Pacific ocean were to be attacked by amphibious forces.

それが「レッド計画」です。この計画では、ハリファクス上陸作戦でカナダへ侵攻し、英本国へは化学兵器による空襲を行い、太平洋の英領諸島に上陸部隊を送り込む予定でした。

The US Navy was to engage the British fleet in the North Atlantic, and prevent British reinforcement of Canada.

第4章　第二次大戦の直前、米国は英国と戦争しようとしていた

　さらに、米海軍は北大西洋上で英海軍を迎え撃ち、カナダへの増援を阻止することになっていました。

　The plan was approved by Army general Douglas MacArthur.

　この計画は、ダグラス・マッカーサー将軍も承認しています。

　Americans were resentful of the British Empire after the First World War, since they had borrowed much money from America, which they did not pay back.

　第一次世界大戦後、米国人は大英帝国に対して憤慨していました。米国から多額の借金をしておきながら、英国が返済しなかったからです。

　Americans are always fearful. In 1935 a certain Captain H. L. George testified to Congress on the danger that Canada posed. He said that since Canada had thousands of natural lakes, these could be used as thousands of float plane bases from which fleets of Canadian aircraft would bomb American cities, railroads, and refineries.

　米国人はいつも恐れています。1935年、H・L・ジョージ大尉が議会でカナダの危険性について証言しました。大尉は、カナダには数千の湖があり、それを水上機の基地として使用されれば、何千もの水上機で米国の大都市、鉄道、製油所などが空襲されてしまう、と述べました。

　He was complimented by several Congressmen for his presentation. The facts are, Canada simply did not have fleets of planes. Float planes of the time could not carry much in the way of a bomb load. And since the floats limit the maneuverability of the aircraft, such planes were at an extreme disadvantage in aerial combat at that time.

　この彼の証言を支持する議員たちもいました。しかし実際は、カ

Chapter4 America desired war with Great Britain just before WWII

ナダにはそんな大規模な航空部隊などなく、しかも、当時の水上機は搭載量が少ないので、大して爆弾を搭載できませんでした。それに、水上機には大きなフロートがついているので、運動性能が低く、空中戦になったら簡単に撃墜されてしまいます。

This is some reality. But at the time, many Americans were terrified of the danger of Great Britain and Canada. Even though there was no such danger.

それが事実でした。しかし当時、多くの米国人は、危険性など全くないのにもかかわらず、カナダと英国を恐れていました。

In May 1930 War Plan Red was approved by Secretary of War Patrick J. Hurley and Secretary of the Navy Charles Adams III.

1930年5月、このレッド計画は、パトリック・J・ハーリー陸軍長官とチャールズ・フランシス・アダムス3世海軍長官の承認を受けました。

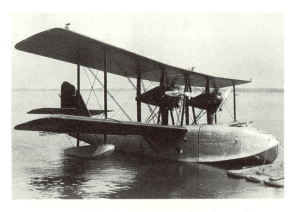

A representative 1930's Canadian Vickers flying boat at Vancouver.
1930年代のカナダ空軍の飛行艇、カナディアン・ヴィッカース・ヴァンクーヴァー

第 4 章　第二次大戦の直前、米国は英国と戦争しようとしていた

The plan was to use a poison gas attack on Halifax, and land troops there. In 1934 plans were updated to make as much use of chemical weapons as possible. Troops were to seize power plants at Niagara Falls.

この計画では、まずカナダのハリファクスに毒ガス攻撃を加え、その後、部隊が上陸します。1934 年には、さらに大量の化学兵器を使用するものに計画が更新され、部隊はナイアガラの滝の発電所を占拠することになっていました。

57 million dollars was approved to build 3 airfields disguised as civilian airports to bomb Canada, troops and military supplies were gathered in Fort Drum, New York.

カナダ空襲に必要な、民間空港に擬装した 3 カ所の飛行場を建設するための 5700 万ドルの予算が認められ、部隊と軍需品がニューヨーク州フォート・ドラムに集められました。

The airfield plans were published on the front page of The New York Times of May 1, 1935.

この飛行場計画は、1935 年 5 月 1 日のニューヨーク・タイムズ第一面に掲載されています。

America feared a war against Great Britain allied with Japan. As such, War Plan Red-Orange was created.

米国はまた、日本の同盟国である英国と戦争になることを恐れていたため、「レッド・オレンジ計画」を作成しました。

Despite the efforts of Prime Minister Konoe to meet American demands, he was rebuffed by America. America wanted war to destroy Japan. America also wanted to destroy Germany and Great Britain. This is because these countries existed.

近衛文麿総理大臣が米国の要求に応えようと努力したにもかかわ

Chapter4 America desired war with Great Britain just before WWII

らず、米国からすげなく断られます。米国は、戦争によって日本を滅亡させることを望んでいました。また米国は、英国とドイツの滅亡も望んでいました。それらの国が「存在すること」が、その理由です。

Today, they fight among themselves, destroying their own nation.

その米国は現在、内乱状態にあり、今度は自分で自分の国を滅ぼそうとしています。

Prime Minister Prince Konoe Fumimaro.

近衛文麿首相

Chapter 5
Why was Japan not colonized?
なぜ日本は植民地にならなかったのか？

The coming of Perry to Japan and the American Civil war
ペリー来航と南北戦争

Japanese people, after 70 years of close relations with America, have no idea of the rapaciousness and acquisitiveness of Americans, and Westerners in general. When you talk to an American, they always show off their possessions. If you visit an American town, the most renowned person is not the person with the deepest knowledge or experience, but the richest person.

日本人は戦後70年間、米国と緊密な関係にありましたが、米国人、西洋人の富に対する貪欲さを理解していません。米国人と話をすると、彼らは常に自分の所有物、財産を自慢します。米国の街を訪問するとよく分かりますが、最も名声のある人物は、知識や経験の豊富な人ではなく、一番の金持ちです。

When Commodore Perry came to Japan to force trade agreements, there are some Japanese people who describe this action as a polite door knock.

ペリー提督は通商条約を強要するために日本にやってきましたが、この時ペリーは「礼儀正しくドアをノックした」と言う日本人がいます。

Not at all. He arrived with four warships, so his intentions were not at

Chapter 5 Why was Japan not colonized?

all peaceful. And 6 months later when he returned for an answer to his demands, he had 9 warships. He left no doubt that force would be used if Japan did not accede to his demands.

それは全然違います。彼は軍艦4隻でやってきましたが、その意図は全く平和的なものではありませんでした。半年後、日本側の返答を聞くために戻ってきた時、軍艦は9隻に増えていました。日本が米国の要求に同意しなかった場合、間違いなく武力が行使されていたでしょう。

Commodore Matthew Perry.

マシュー・ペリー提督

He also proposed to then President Pierce that America annex the Ryukyu islands as a protectorate, along with Formosa (now Taiwan). The President said no.

さらにペリー提督は、当時のピアース大統領に対して、米国が琉球王国と台湾を保護領として併合することを提案しています。しかし大統領の返事は「ノー」でした。

There are people who say Japan was not colonized because there were no resources worth the trouble. No. Here, geography helped Japan. The European powers came from the West. France in Vietnam, the Dutch in what is now Indonesia, and the British in Malaysia and Hong Kong.

第 5 章　なぜ日本は植民地にならなかったのか？

　日本が植民地にされなかったのは資源がなかったからだ、という人がいます。いいえ、そうではありません。それよりも、地理的な要因が大きかったのです。ヨーロッパの国々は西方からやってきて、フランスはベトナム、オランダは現在のインドネシア、英国はマレーシアと香港を植民地化しました。

The Spanish Empire had already passed the peak of it's power, and given up on the concept of colonizing Japan.

　スペイン帝国はその絶頂期をとうに過ぎ、日本を植民地にするという構想をあきらめていました。

These countries were all small in population, and the dominance of these vast territories took much national energy.

　これらの国々は人口が少なかったため、この広大な地域を支配するには多大な国力を必要としました。

America was late on the scene in Asia. Except for Thailand and Japan, everywhere else was already taken into possession by other European nations. China was being carved up into spheres of influence by European powers.

　一方の米国はアジアへの進出に出遅れていました。すでに、タイと日本以外の国々は全て他のヨーロッパ諸国が支配しており、中国はヨーロッパ諸国によって分割されていました。

America had only gained access to the Pacific ocean in 1848, with victory in the war against Mexico. No time was wasted in sending Commodore Perry on a military expedition to dominate Japan.

　1848 年、メキシコとの米墨戦争に勝利した後、米国はようやく太平洋に進出しました。そして早速、日本を支配するためにペリー提督を送りました。

Chapter5 Why was Japan not colonized?

What saved Japan from being colonized by America was the American Civil War. It distracted America long enough that the Meiji revolution could get started, and a strong central authority with a national Army and Navy could be established. This made colonizing Japan too difficult for America.

日本が米国の植民地にならずにすんだのは、南北戦争によるところが大きかったと言えます。米国がこの国内問題にかかりきりになっている間に、日本は明治維新によって、強い中央政府、および海軍と陸軍を設立しました。これで、米国が日本を植民地化することが困難になりました。

By the time the American Civil War was over, the American west coast was not developed enough to support an invasion of Japan. Japan was very lucky.

南北戦争が終わった頃、米国の西海岸はまだ、日本への侵略計画を支援できるほど開発が進んでいませんでした。日本は運がよかったのです。

Both Portugal and Spain desired Japan but were thwarted when the Tokugawa unified the country. Western writers portray the Closed Country policy as weakness, but the Tokugawa simply did not wish to deal with Westerners.

かつてポルトガルとスペインが共に日本の支配を狙っていましたが、徳川幕府が国を統一したためにできなくなりました。西洋人の歴史家は、鎖国を間違った政策のように語りますが、徳川幕府は単に、西洋人と関わりたくなかったのです。

Chapter 6

The war that did not happen, the Tokugawa Shogunate attacks, defeats the Spanish Empire, annexes the Philippines

実現しなかった戦争、徳川幕府がスペインに勝利し、フィリピンを併合

A simulation of a war between Tokugawa Japan and Spain
日本vsスペインというシミュレーション

I think that Westerners simply could not comprehend the closed country policy. When confronted with a nation they do not like, Westerners, instead of shutting themselves off, would attack.

西洋人には、日本のとった鎖国政策は理解できないでしょう。なぜなら西洋人は、嫌な国が現れた時、鎖国ではなく、攻撃するからです。

So what if the Tokugawa, instead of closing the country, decided to attack Spain? Frankly, the Philippines could have been easily conquered by the Tokugawa government.

そこで、もし徳川幕府が、鎖国をせずにスペインを攻撃していたら、どうなっていたでしょうか？ 率直に言うと、徳川幕府はフィリピンを簡単に征服していたでしょう。

Spanish forces in the Philippines would have been few. There was a yearly galleon to Mexico. Perhaps we could imagine a couple of galleons based in the Philippines. These were the primary large warships of the

Chapter6　The war that did not happen, the Tokugawa Shogunate attacks, defeats the Spanish Empire, annexes the Philippines

A Spanish Galleon.

スペインのガリオン船

day. And a land force of some thousands could have been stationed in the Philippines.

　フィリピンには、スペインの軍事力は大してありませんでした。一年に一度、ガリオン船がメキシコに出帆していたので、フィリピンに拠点をおくガリオン船は数隻あったと考えられます。このガリオン船は当時、主力の大型軍艦でした。それに加えて、地上部隊が数千人はいたでしょう。

However, the Tokugawa of say, the year 1630, could easily muster some 100,000 warriors. More forces probably. Along with forces of the outer Barons, defeated at Sekigahara, another 50,000 could have been sent.

　しかし、当時の徳川幕府は、例えば1630年の時点なら、容易に10万人の武士を招集できました。関ヶ原で負けた西軍でも、5万人は集められるでしょう。

And infantry weaponry and artillery for Japanese armies of the time were comparable to what Spain had.

第 6 章　実現しなかった戦争、徳川幕府がスペインに勝利し、フィリピンを併合

　また、当時の日本の歩兵の武装や大砲の質は、スペインのものと同等でした。

At that time, there were some 350 Japanese Red Seal Ships. They were 500 to 750 tons, with 6 or 8 guns, compared to a Spanish galleon of 1,000 tons. A Manila galleon would be up to 2,000 tons. Spanish galleons carried on average about 20 to 30 guns.

　一方、当時の日本は朱印船を 350 隻ほど保有していました。船の大きさは 500 から 750 トンで、それぞれ 6 〜 8 門の大砲を装備していました。それに対して、スペインのガリオン船が千トン、マニラ・ガリオン（メキシコへの連絡船）は 2 千トンでした。スペインのガリオン船は 20 〜 30 門の大砲を搭載していました。

Japanese people are a hard working and innovative race. I have no doubt that if the need was there, larger warships would have been built, say 20 guns or more.

A typical Japanese Red Seal ship.

日本の朱印船

Chapter6　The war that did not happen, the Tokugawa Shogunate attacks, defeats the Spanish Empire, annexes the Philippines

　それでも、日本人は巧みに創意工夫する民族です。必要があれば、もっと大きい船、例えば20門の大砲を搭載した船を造っていたのは間違いありません。

However, with the larger Spanish galleons, there would only be at most a few such ships in Philippine waters at any given time. In the attempted invasion of England by the Spanish Armada of 1588, the English ships were smaller than the Spanish. But they were much more maneuverable, and the Spanish fleet failed in it's objective of invading England.

　しかも、スペインの大型ガリオン船は、フィリピン海域には数隻しかありません。1588年のスペイン無敵艦隊による英国侵攻では、迎え撃った英国海軍の船はスペインの船より小さいものでした。けれどもスペインの船よりはるかに機動性にすぐれていたため、スペイン艦隊の英国侵略計画は失敗に終わりました。

The Philippines are a long way away from the home country of Spain. It was a 4 month voyage to Mexico. From there, cross Mexico, and take ship for Spain. A one way trip would take some 8 or 9 months. Most likely more. And of course, that would be the speed of a message to the Spanish King that there was war with Japan in the Philippines.

　フィリピンは、スペイン本国から遠く離れています。フィリピンからメキシコまでの航海は4カ月かかります。そこから、メキシコを横断し、スペインまで船で向かえば、片道で合計8～9カ月はかかるでしょう。もっとかかるかもしれません。スペイン王へのメッセージ、例えば「フィリピンで日本とスペインの戦争が始まった」という知らせを届けるのにも、同じ月日がかかります。

At the time, Spain was already in Imperial overstretch. Also there was a serious pirate problem in the Caribbean sea. This required many galleons to convoy gold from Mexico and South America to Spain. This left fewer ships able to protect the Philippines.

第6章　実現しなかった戦争、徳川幕府がスペインに勝利し、フィリピンを併合

　当時、スペイン帝国は、勢力を拡げすぎているという問題がありました。また、カリブ海で海賊に襲われるという問題があり、メキシコや南米からスペインまで金を輸送するのに、多くのガリオン船が必要となりました。そのせいで、フィリピン防衛に使えるガリオン船の数は少なくなります。

The Philippines was at the farthest point of the Empire from Spain.

　フィリピンは、スペイン本国から最も遠いところにありました。

So if a Japanese army under the Tokugawa with a fleet of such Red Seal Ships attacked, they would be able to land many tens of thousands of troops. A number of Red Seal Ships would be lost attacking the galleons, but in the end, damage of things like a rudder, or maneuvering the Spanish ship into dangerous waters with reefs, one by one the Spanish vessels would be overcome.

　つまり、徳川幕府の朱印船の艦隊は、何万人もの兵士を上陸させてフィリピンを攻撃することが可能でした。ガリオン船との海戦で朱印船を何隻か失うかもしれませんが、最終的にはスペインのガリオン船も徐々にダメージを受け、また危険な珊瑚礁の水域に誘い込まれて、一隻ずつ戦闘能力を喪失していくでしょう。

On land, there were some very extensive fortresses, for example Intramuros, on Fort Santiago in present Manila. But these fortresses could be overcome by siege warfare. It would take some 2 years, or more, for Spain to be able to send a force to counter-attack Japan.

　一方、陸上には、例えば現在のマニラのイントラムロス、サンチャゴに大要塞がありました。しかし、これらの要塞を包囲して陥落させることは可能です。スペイン本国から増援が到着するまでには、少なくとも2年、あるいはそれ以上の時間がかかります。

The Spanish land forces would be greatly outnumbered by the

Chapter6　The war that did not happen, the Tokugawa Shogunate attacks, defeats the Spanish Empire, annexes the Philippines

Tokugawa Army in every location. There is a basic rule of land combat. In open terrain, you need numbers of 3 to 1 to have a reasonable chance of victory.

こうして、あらゆる場所で、徳川軍はスペインの地上軍よりも兵力が大幅に上回ります。地上戦において、一つの基本的な法則があります。敵に勝つためには３倍の兵力が必要、ということです。

The Japanese troops would be of superior quality and would outnumber the Spanish. The only Spanish choice would be to withdraw into their fortresses.

日本の武士は、スペインの兵士より質、量ともに上回っていました。スペインの選択肢は一つしかありません。要塞に立て籠もることです。

Also, Bushido, the Japanese philosophy of the road of the warrior, would have been a serious factor in any war with Spain. This is a unique philosophy among nations. With this philosophy, Japan had the strongest infantry in the world at that time.

それと、武士道の精神は、このスペインとの戦争において、重要な因子となるでしょう。そのような価値観を持っているのは、世界の中で日本だけであり、そのような日本の武士は、当時世界最強の歩兵でした。

In addition, Japan, being geographically closer, would have the advantage. I think the Spanish would have made one serious effort to counter attack. Perhaps even landing a force somewhere in mainland Japan. But this force would have lacked support from the Spanish homeland because Spain was too distant. The Spanish would have been defeated in the end.

日本が地理的に近いことも有利です。日本が攻めてくれば、スペ

第 6 章　実現しなかった戦争、徳川幕府がスペインに勝利し、フィリピンを併合

インは全力で反撃しようとするでしょう。もしかしたら、日本のどこかに上陸してくるかもしれません。しかし、スペイン本国は遠すぎて、この上陸部隊は本国からの支援が得られません。となれば結局、この部隊は撃退されることになるでしょう。

In 1582, in the siege of Takamatsu castle, a dam was built, flooding the castle and forcing it to surrender. This shows that Japanese forces were quite innovative in siege warfare.

例えば 1582 年にあった備中高松城の攻城戦では、秀吉は堤防を造って城を水攻めにし、降伏させました。こうしたことによっても、日本軍の攻城戦がとても革新的だったことが分かります。

The Spanish fortifications in the Philippines would have had to hold out for at least 2 years before relief could come from Spain. Two years is a long time, it is doubtful that enough food could be gathered for the garrison to last that long. The Japanese forces would have access to food from the countryside.

さて、フィリピンにあるスペインの要塞に立て籠もった後、兵士たちはスペインから増援が来るまで、少なくとも 2 年は耐えなければなりません。しかしこうした守備隊が 2 年分もの食糧を備蓄することはできないでしょう。一方の日本軍は、要塞の外で自由に食糧を調達できます。

If we assume an invading Japanese force of 100,000, it would take some 300,000 Spanish troops to defeat them. This is that military rule of thumb, that on level ground, to win in combat you need at least 3 times the troops of your opponent.

仮に日本軍が 10 万人だと仮定すると、スペイン軍は少なくとも 30 万人が必要になります。これは先述のように、軍事的な経験則から、少なくとも地上戦で勝利するには敵軍の 3 倍の兵力が必要だ

からです。

In Spain's attempted invasion of Great Britain in 1588 the ships carried some 18,000 infantry. And by 1630, the Spanish Navy had shrunk very much since 1588.

先ほどの 1588 年の英国への侵略計画では、スペイン艦隊は 1 万 8 千名の歩兵を運びました。しかし 1630 年には、スペイン艦隊の軍艦数はずっと減少していました。

They would not be able to transport enough troops to retake the Philippines, and the archipelago would have fallen to Japan.

つまり、スペインはフィリピンを奪回するだけの兵力を輸送することは不可能であり、フィリピン群島は全て日本の手に落ちるのです。

Furthermore England would have made a natural ally of Japan. By about 1640, the Philippines would have become an integral part of Japan. And this is the reason why Spain never attacked Japan after the closing of the country.

そして、英国と日本は必然的に同盟関係となり、1640 年頃までには、フィリピンは日本の領土になっていたでしょう。そういう状況にあったので、スペインは鎖国後の日本を攻撃しなかったのです。

The use of missionaries as an excuse for invasion
宣教師を利用した侵略

Missionaries were commonly used as an excuse to conquer a country by Europeans. The process went like this -- Missionaries arrive and exploit social problems in a country. They then create further social turmoil.

第６章　実現しなかった戦争、徳川幕府がスペインに勝利し、フィリピンを併合

　ヨーロッパ人は他国を征服するのに、宣教師を利用していました。それは以下のようなプロセスです。まず、宣教師がある国に到着した後、その国の社会問題を利用し、その問題をさらに大きくして、社会を混乱させます。

The country then kills the missionaries. The missionaries home country then invades to punish that country for killing it's missionaries, and takes it over. That country then becomes a colony.

　すると、その国は社会を混乱させた宣教師を殺します。次に、宣教師を送り込んだ本国は、宣教師が殺されたことを口実にその国を侵略し、征服してしまいます。その国は植民地になります。

In the era of warring states, when missionaries began to arrive in Japan, Japan was in civil war, with many local leaders, or feudal Barons, vying for power.

　宣教師が到着し始めた戦国時代の日本は、群雄割拠し、内戦が続いていました。

It was an ideal situation for a European nation to conquer through it's missionaries. The missionaries concentrated their efforts on converting Barons in Western Japan.

　つまり、ヨーロッパの国が宣教師を使って征服をするのに理想的な状況でした。そこで宣教師たちは、西日本の大名たちを改宗させることに力を集中しました。

When the decision to close the country and expel foreign missionaries came, Japanese domestic Christians were forced to renounce Christianity or be killed. This would have been an excuse for the Spanish to invade Japan. Why? Well to protect Christian believers. This is how Westerners think, plan, and use people.

Chapter6　The war that did not happen, the Tokugawa Shogunate attacks, defeats the Spanish Empire, annexes the Philippines

　日本が鎖国して外国人宣教師の追放が決まると、日本人のキリスト教徒は信仰を放棄するか、あるいは殺されるか、という状況になりました。これは、スペインが日本を侵略する口実にできます。キリスト教の信者を守るため、という名目が得られるからです。西洋人はこのように考え、計画し、人々を利用します。

However Japan under the Tokugawa was much too militarily powerful for Spain to invade, so they did not. If Japan at the time was politically united, but without strong military power, Japan would have been overrun by the Spanish and Christianized. Buddhism and Shintoism would have been abolished with Japan turned into a slave nation under Spanish rule.

　しかし、徳川幕府下の日本は、強力な軍隊をもっていたので、スペインは侵略してきませんでした。たとえ当時の日本が統一国家であったとしても、強い軍事力がなければ、スペインに蹂躙されていたでしょう。そして、日本は仏教と神道が廃止され、キリスト教の国となり、スペインが支配する奴隷国家になっていたでしょう。

What would such a Japan have been like? Look at Mexico and Peru today, along with other South and Central American nations. In Mexico, the Indian Aztec Empire existed, along with the Inca Empire in Peru. The Spanish exploited political divisions with Indian tribes opposed to the Aztecs and took over the entire country.

　その場合、日本はどんな国になっていたでしょうか？　現在のメキシコやペルー、他の中南米の国を見てください。メキシコにはアステカ帝国があり、ペルーにはインカ帝国がありました。スペインは、アステカとそれに敵対する部族間の政治問題を利用して、全土を乗っ取ってしまいました。

And Spain took over the Inca Empire. Today, the descendants of Central American Indians are generally poor, and second class. People of mixed and Spanish blood, and some pure blood Spanish descended people

第6章　実現しなかった戦争、徳川幕府がスペインに勝利し、フィリピンを併合

are the richer and upper classes to this day.

　さらにインカ帝国もスペインに征服されました。現在、中央アメリカの原住民の子孫は、だいたいが貧しい、下層階級です。一方で、スペイン人との混血や純粋なスペイン系の子孫は今も豊かで、上流階級です。

Japan was saved from such a fate by having a powerful military.

日本は、強い軍隊があったおかげで、そういうことにならずにすんだわけです。

In Japan today, people who oppose changing Article 9 of the Constitution argue that to have a military means to wage war. So they say that Japan should not have a military. Yet if this is true, why did the Tokugawa not attack Spain?

Spanish forces assaulting the Aztec capital of Tenochtitlan.
アステカ王国の首都テノチティトランに攻め込むスペイン軍

Chapter6　The war that did not happen, the Tokugawa Shogunate attacks, defeats the Spanish Empire, annexes the Philippines

今の日本で、憲法9条の改正に反対する人たちは、「軍隊があると戦争になる」と主張しています。「だから、日本は軍隊を持ってはならない」と言います。しかし、それが本当なら、なぜ徳川幕府はスペインと戦争をしなかったのでしょうか？

Spain's and Portugal's goal was to use the Barons to create Spanish and Portuguese colonies in Japan itself. But they did not possess the military power to do this. Spain and Portugal both irritated Japan by gaining influence with Japan's Western Feudal Barons.

こうしたスペインやポルトガルの目標は、日本に植民地を作ることでした。しかし、自分たちでそれを実行する軍事力はありません。スペインとポルトガルの両国は、戦国時代の西日本の大名に影響力を行使し、幕府と対立するように仕向けました。

A Christian Baron, Otomo Sorin.

キリシタン大名、大友宗麟

So they converted some Western Barons to Christianity, and hoped to use them as proxies in talking over Japan. When the Western Baron's were defeated at Sekigahara in 1600, the colonization of Japan became impossible.

そこで彼らは、西の大名を何人かキリスト教に改宗させ、日本支配の代理人として利用するつもりでした。しかし1600年の関ヶ原の戦いで西軍が負けたので、日本の植民地化は不可能になりました。

第 6 章　実現しなかった戦争、徳川幕府がスペインに勝利し、フィリピンを併合

Eventually Christianity was stamped out and forced underground in Japan. But the Tokugawa were not interested in a Pacific-wide Empire, and so they closed themselves off.

そのうちにキリスト教は禁止され、キリシタンは潜伏することになりました。しかし、徳川幕府は太平洋に覇権を求めることには関心がなく、鎖国をしました。

And a closed-off Japan was too militarily powerful to be invaded outright, so the Spanish and Portuguese gave up.

鎖国した日本を侵略するにはその軍事力は強大すぎて、スペインとポルトガルは日本への侵攻をあきらめました。

It is interesting to imagine how history would be different if Japan had conquered the Philippines, and raised the people there up to standards of Japanese civilization.

もし日本がフィリピンを征服し、フィリピンの文明を日本の水準にまで引き上げていたら、歴史はどう変わっていたでしょうか。そういうことを想像するのも面白いです。

Americans only think of themselves
米国人は自分たちのことしか考えていない

The difference in WWII was that when Commodore Perry arrived in 1853, he had advanced military technology. Japanese military forces had not changed much since 1600. So America could force Japan to agree to demands with superior weaponry.

大東亜戦争の日米開戦時と違うのは、1853年にペリー提督が日本にやってきた時、彼は当時の最先端の軍事技術を持っていたこと

です。日本の武器は1600年の時からあまり進歩していませんでした。それで、最先端の兵器を持っていた米国は、自分たちの要求を呑むよう強制することができました。

In those days, colonies were the only way for an industrial country to survive.

当時、工業国が存続するためには、植民地を持つしかありませんでした。

The present Japanese Constitution has done nothing to protect Japan. And America has not done much either. It was forced upon Japan by an enemy nation: the United States of America.

現在の日本国憲法は、日本を守るのに何の役にも立っていません。米国も日本を守るつもりで日本にいるわけではありません。憲法は、当時敵国だった米国が、日本に強制したものです。

The major reason for the American bases to be in Japan is not to protect Japan, but to project American power into other countries. America depended on bases in Japan in the Vietnam war, and depends on them now in sending troops to the Middle East.

日本に米軍基地がある理由は、日本を守るためではなく、米国の軍事力を他の地域に展開するための拠点として必要だからです。ベトナム戦争では、米国は日本の基地が必要でしたし、現在は、中東に軍を派遣するのに必要です。

Yes, at present Japan and the United States have a good relationship. And more and more Americans do like and trust Japan. My estimation now is about 20% of Americans actually like Japan. But most Americans don't trust Japan.

もちろん現在、日本と米国は良好な関係にあります。日本を好き

第6章　実現しなかった戦争、徳川幕府がスペインに勝利し、フィリピンを併合

で、信頼するという米国人が増えています。私の推定では、現在約2割の米国人が日本に好意的です。しかし、それでもまだ大多数の米国人は、日本を信頼していません。

Well, most Americans don't like any other country, they are too involved with themselves.

まあ、ほとんどの米国人は、日本に限らず、よその国が好きではありません。彼らは、自分たちのことにしか関心がないのです。

But it is very naive of Japanese people to think of America as a benevolent elder brother. America moves solely for it's own profit. If letting another nation attack Japan was profitable, they would easily let it happen.

US Marine base, Camp Hansen.
米海兵隊の基地、キャンプ・ハンセン

Chapter 6 The war that did not happen, the Tokugawa Shogunate attacks, defeats the Spanish Empire, annexes the Philippines

しかし、日本人が米国を優しいお兄さんのような国であると考えるのは、あまりにも現実を知らなさすぎです。米国は自分たちの利益のためにしか動きません。もし、他国が日本を攻撃して米国が利益を得られるのであれば、米国は容易に、そうなるように仕向けるでしょう。

At the end of WWII, Japan was still an enemy of America. The occupation reformed Japan to bring Japan under American power, and to ensure that Japan would never be strong again.

終戦時、米国はまだ日本の敵国でした。占領時代に米国が行った日本の改革は、日本を米国の支配下におき、日本が再び強い国にならないようにするためのものでした。

Japanese people don't understand what war and occupation really mean. In the Warring States Era, the ruling lord of a fief could be defeated in battle, and his castle and fief taken over by another lord. But for the townspeople and farmers, life would go on as usual.

日本人は、戦争や占領というものが、実際どういうものか分かっていません。戦国時代は、ある藩の大名が戦で負けると、別の大名がそのお城と藩を引き継ぎ、町人や農民の生活には、あまり変化がありませんでした。

In all other nations in the world, they would have been enslaved or exterminated. The American occupation of Japan was more benign than most occupations, but still American soldiers committed many crimes with impunity.

しかし、他の国は違います。戦争に負けた国の国民は、皆殺しにされるか、奴隷になるかです。米国兵は日本で数多くの犯罪を犯し、しかも罪に問われることはありませんでしたが、それでも米国による日本の占領は、他国の占領政策よりも、ずっとましなものでした。

第 6 章　実現しなかった戦争、徳川幕府がスペインに勝利し、フィリピンを併合

The first Sino-Japanese war and the Russo-Japanese war that surprised the world
世界を驚かせた日清・日露戦争

If having a standing Army means that you automatically start wars, then Tokugawa Japan would have indeed attacked Spain simply because Spain was weak in Asia. Instead, what Tokugawa Japan did was unique in history.

もし国が軍隊を持つと自動的に戦争を始めるのであれば、徳川幕府は絶対にスペインを攻撃したでしょう。なぜなら、アジアではスペインは強大な存在ではなかったからです。でも徳川幕府は、それをしませんでした。そして、徳川幕府が実際にとった政策は、世界史上、類のないものでした。

Not wanting to get involved with Westerners and their problems, Japan closed itself off. And at that time Japan had the military power to keep Western countries at bay.

西洋人や彼らが持ち込む面倒な問題に関わりたくなかったので、日本は鎖国しました。そして当時の日本には、西洋から自国を守るだけの軍事力がありました。

When the Americans arrived in 1853, they were too militarily powerful to ignore. They arrived in coal powered steam vessels, that could move against the wind. To survive, Japan had to adopt this technology.

しかし 1853 年に米国人が日本にやってきた時、その軍事力は強大で、日本はそれを無視できませんでした。彼らの軍艦は、石炭を燃料とする蒸気船で、風に逆らって移動することができました。日本が生き残るためには、この技術を習得する必要がありました。

Chapter6　The war that did not happen, the Tokugawa Shogunate attacks, defeats the Spanish Empire, annexes the Philippines

And Japan did adopt Western military technology. Japan modernized with a rapidity that amazed the world, no other country has done anything similar.

そして、日本は西洋の技術を習得し、世界が驚くほどの速さで近代化を成し遂げました。他の国ではこのような例がありません。

And this is why Western countries fear Japan, even today.

そのため、現在でも、西洋諸国は日本を恐れているのです。

Japan then began several wars of survival. The First Sino-Japanese War of 1894 to 1895 was to demonstrate that Japan, not China would be the leader of Asia.

Commodore Perry's flagship USS Susquehanna.
ペリー提督が座乗していたサスケハナ号

第6章 実現しなかった戦争、徳川幕府がスペインに勝利し、フィリピンを併合

　その後、日本は何度か、その生存をかけて戦争を始めました。日清戦争（1894-1895）では、アジアの指導国は中国ではなく日本であることを証明しました。

This was very similar to the war against the Austria-Hungarian Empire by Prussia in 1866. That was to ensure that Prussia, not Austria-Hungary, would dominate the German states.

　これは、1866年のプロシア対オーストリア・ハンガリー帝国の戦争とよく似ています。この戦争は、オーストリア・ハンガリー帝国ではなく、プロシアがドイツを支配するリーダーであることを明確に示しました。

The Russo-Japanese War of 1904 to 1905 amazed the world. Since ending the Closed Country Policy when Commodore Perry arrived, Japan was able to build a military that could defeat a Western Christian power -- Russia -- at war. In only 51 years, Japan went from a technologically backward nation to a technologically advanced country. It also terrified Western countries.

　日露戦争(1904-1905)は、世界を驚かせました。ペリー来航によって開国した日本は、西洋キリスト教国と戦争して勝てる軍隊を持つに至りました。わずか51年で、後進国から先進国に変身したのです。これによって、西洋列強は日本を恐れるようになりました。

Japan then established the nation of Manchukuo, and invaded China to establish security in a chaotic nation.

　その後、日本は満洲国を造り、国家の安全を確保するために中国と衝突し、侵攻しました。

And then following extreme American provocation, attacked American, British and Dutch possessions in Asia.

Chapter6 The war that did not happen, the Tokugawa Shogunate attacks, defeats the Spanish Empire, annexes the Philippines

そして米国から度を超した挑発行為を受け、アジアにある米英蘭の植民地を攻撃することになったのです。

Many people in Japan today think this was unreasonable aggression. Not at all. People might say that Japan should have been conciliatory to please foreigners.

今の日本では、多くの人が、日本はバカげた侵略戦争をしたと思っています。しかしそれは全く違います。彼らはおそらく、日本は外国の人たちが満足するような融和政策をとればよかったのに、と言うのでしょう。

No. The only way to please foreigners who criticize Japan is commit suicide or to submit to slavery. These Japanese people who think like this do not understand the true nature of foreigners.

でも、そんなことはできません。日本を非難する外国人を満足させる方法は、二つだけです。自害するか、奴隷となって服従するかです。そんなことを考えている日本人は、外国人の本質を全く分かっていないのです。

第7章　日本が植民地になっていたら、どうなっていたか

Chapter 7
What life would have been like if Japan had been colonized
日本が植民地になっていたら、どうなっていたか

Looking at the colonial policy of Imperial Briton
英国のインド支配に見る植民地政策

Let us take a look at what Japan would have be like today if Japan did not fight. Let us imagine that President Roosevelt had accepted Prime Minister Konoe's offer of peace.

では、もし日本が大東亜戦争を戦わなかったら、今の日本はどうなっていたでしょうか。ルーズベルト大統領が近衛首相の講和提案を受諾した場合を想像してみてください。

One of those conditions was that Japan withdraw the Imperial Army from northern China. Gradually, America would have applied economic pressure until Japan was helpless. This could have been easily done by limiting the amount of oil sold to Japan.

米国の条件の一つは、日本陸軍の北支からの撤退でした。そこで米国は、刃向かう力がなくなるまで、日本に経済的圧力をかけ続けていたでしょう。これは、日本に輸出する石油に制限をかけることで、容易に実行できます。

Over some years, political pressure would have been applied to reduce the Japanese military. American companies would have applied political pressure to gain control of Japanese industries.

Chapter7 What life would have been like if Japan had been colonized

　その後、日本の軍事力を弱体化させるために、数年にわたって政治的な圧力が加えられたでしょう。また、米国の企業が日本の企業を支配下に置くための政治的な圧力も加えられていたでしょう。

　Gradually, over a few years, Japanese people would have become second-class citizens in Japan. Japan would have looked a lot like India colonized by Great Britain.

　こうして日本人は、数年の間に二等国の国民になっていきます。日本は、英国が植民地化したインドのようになるでしょう。

　Places like the Hakone resort area, Karuizawa, the Imperial hotel in Tokyo, could only be entered by Japanese people as servants. These places would have been reserved for the American elite.

　箱根のリゾート地、軽井沢、東京の帝国ホテルのようなところにいる日本人は、使用人だけです。こういう場所は、米国のエリートたちだけが利用できるようになります。

President Franklin Roosevelt.
フランクリン・ルーズベルト大統領

第 7 章　日本が植民地になっていたら、どうなっていたか

Japanese would work for American companies at pittance wages. Draconian laws would regulate the movement of people in the country. Rivalry between Eastern and Western Japan would be encouraged. Education of children would have been changed regionally to encourage the disunity of Japan.

米国の企業は、日本人を低賃金で労働させます。日本人が自国内を移動するのも、厳しい法律で規制されます。米国は西日本と東日本の対立を煽り、児童に対する教育は、地域ごとに異なる内容に変更されていたでしょう。日本国内での対立を扇動するためです。

For a good example of this, let us look at the British Raj, the British rule of India.

日本で起こることの好例として、実際の、英国によるインド支配を見てみましょう。

One striking example is the Bengal famine of 1943 to 1944. Famines had occasionally happened in Bengal when under Mughal rule. The Mughal government, which taxed the peasantry at 10 to 15%, would waive taxes and take relief measures, such as irrigation.

1943年から1944年まで続いたベンガル飢饉、これがその特筆すべき例です。それ以前、ムガール帝国の支配のもとでも、ベンガルでは時々飢饉が起こりました。ムガール帝国政府は農民の収入に10〜15％の課税をしていましたが、飢饉が起きると政府は税を免除し、灌漑などの救済措置を講じました。

In the 1765 treaty of Allahabad the British East India Company took over taxation from the Mughal Emperor and immediately taxes increased to 50%.

しかし、1765年のアラハバード条約で英国の東インド会社がムガール皇帝から徴税権を引き継ぐと、税率は直ちに50％に引き上げられました。

Chapter7 What life would have been like if Japan had been colonized

When famine came, instead of waiving taxes, the British demanded that surviving farmers make up the balance of farmers who had died. Also, they ordered the planting of cash crops such as Indigo and Poppy that had a high market value, but were inedible in times of famine.

英国は、税収を維持するために、ムガール帝国政府のように飢饉の時に免税するのではなく、飢饉を生き残った農家に減収分を補わせました。また、英国はインディゴやポピーのような換金作物を植えるよう指示しましたが、それらの作物は、市場価値は高くとも、飢饉の時には空腹を満たしません。

In the 1943 famine 3 million people died. Prime Minister Winston Churchill stated that it was their own fault, for breeding like rabbits.

それで、1943年の飢饉では300万人が亡くなりました。しかし英国のウィンストン・チャーチル首相は、飢饉を引き起こしたのはインド人の責任である、ウサギのように繁殖するからだ、と言い放ったのです。

The greed of Western capitalists
強欲な西洋の資本家たち

People in Japan might say that Americans would never be this cruel to Japan, but oh yes they would. How can I say this? Simply look at America today.

日本人は、「だが、米国人がそんなひどいことを日本に対してするはずがない」と言うかもしれませんが、それは違います。ではなぜ私がそう言えるのか？ 今の米国を見てください。

In British India, the British were simply concerned about profit. They did not care about what effect their policies had on the lives of the people who lived in India. The same is true for American Capitalists.

英国植民地時代のインドでは、英国人は自分たちの利益しか考えませんでした。その政策がインドに住んでいる人たちにどんな影響を及ぼすかなど、考えることはなかったのです。しかしこれは、米国の資本家たちも同じです。

They have created a society in America where an extreme transfer of wealth has taken place. Many people cannot survive. Their lives have been devastated by outsourcing, or medical bills that are extremely high even for common ailments.

彼らは、米国でひどい格差社会を作りました。米国に住む多くの人たちは、まともな生活ができていません。彼らは、工場などを海外へ移転するアウトソーシングによって仕事を奪われ、あるいは、ちょっとした病気でも非常に高額な医療費を請求され、生活が立ち行かなくなっています。

That is why common Americans elected Donald Trump to the Presidency, he is hope.

そういう理由で、一般の米国人は大統領選挙でドナルド・トランプ氏に投票しました。トランプは、彼らにとっての希望なのです。

I have detailed this in my book "2nd Civil War: The Battle For America". If American Capitalists have no respect for the lives of Americans, they would think even less of the misery of Japanese people they exploited.

私は前著『米国人が語る 日本人に隠しておけない米国の"崩壊"』の中で、そのことを詳しく書いています。このように米国の資本家は、米国人に対してさえ配慮しないのですから、搾取した日本人がどれだけ不幸になろうが、全く気にも留めないでしょう。

Chapter7 What life would have been like if Japan had been colonized

If Japan had not fought in WWII, that would have been Japan's fate, one of misery.

つまり、もしも日本が大東亜戦争を戦っていなかったら、間違いなく日本は、悲惨な運命をたどっていたことでしょう。

There are people who say that we should communicate and talk to people to avoid war. Japanese people are basically alone in this assumption. You cannot negotiate with someone who desires your destruction.

戦争を避けるために、もっと話し合いをすべきだったと言う人がいます。世界中で、そんなおめでたいことを言うのは日本人だけです。日本を滅ぼそうとしている連中と交渉して、よい結果が得られるはずがないのです。

Western Capitalists desire the complete economic dominance of the entire world, and the destruction of anyone they deem to be in their way. Japanese people look for a way to co-exist. This is a fundamental difference.

西洋の資本家は、全世界を経済的に支配したいと考えています。そして、その支配の邪魔になる者は潰そうとします。一方、日本人の場合は、共存する方法を模索します。両者には、こういう根本的な違いがあるのです。

The Japanese military fought bravely
日本軍は勇敢に戦った

I am convinced that the intensity with which Japan fought in the war led to an occupation that was not as bad as it might have been.

第7章　日本が植民地になっていたら、どうなっていたか

　日本があの戦争を、総力を上げて、死にもの狂いで戦ったから、米国の占領がそれほどひどいものにはならなかったのだと、私は確信しています。

　The truth is, Japan could not win by invading America and destroying it. But they could make destroying Japan very difficult and costly. For this, many Japanese Imperial Army and Imperial Navy soldiers and sailors lost their lives. We should remember their sacrifice.

　実際のところ、日本軍には米国本土に侵攻して屈服させるまでの力はありませんでした。しかし日本軍が頑強に抵抗したことで、米国は、日本を潰滅させるのは非常に困難で、莫大なコストがかかることを理解したのです。そのために、数多くの日本軍の兵士が、その命を捧げました。彼らの犠牲的行為を忘れてはいけません。

　But this was a valid war plan. It came close to success. So many Americans dying in assaulting Japanese held islands in the Pacific had an effect upon the morale of the American people. They began to desire peace.

　日本の戦い方は、効果的なものでした。実際、あと少しで成功するところまでいっていたのです。日本軍が立て籠もる島に米軍が上陸し、数多くの米国兵が戦死しましたが、それは米国民の戦意にも影響を及ぼしました。早く戦争をやめたいと考える米国民が増えていったのです。

　The movie "Flags of our Fathers" illustrates this. It shows the great propaganda effort by the American government. American people had to be pressured to continue the war.

　そこで米国政府は、戦争を継続するために、強力なプロパガンダで米国民の厭戦気分を払拭し、戦意を高揚させる必要がありました。クリント・イーストウッド監督の映画「父親たちの星条旗」にも、

Chapter7 What life would have been like if Japan had been colonized

そのことが描かれています。

At the battle of Leyte gulf, Japan came close to success. The Japanese plan worked brilliantly, until Admiral Kurita at the critical moment turned his fleet away.

また、レイテ沖海戦は、成功まであと少しというところまでいきました。日本軍の作戦に、米軍は見事にひっかかりましたが、いちばん重要な段階で、栗田中将がレイテ湾突入を中止し、艦隊を反転させてしまいました。

The stars and stripes on Iwo Jima. Raising the stars and stripes on the meat grinder of Mount Suribachi, these Marines became hero of the nation, they toured the nation in support of the stagnating war bond campaign, doubling the sales goal.

硫黄島の星条旗。激戦の硫黄島、摺り鉢山山頂に星条旗を立てた海兵隊員たちは、低迷していた戦時国債のキャンペーンのため全米を回り、目標額の２倍を売り上げる成功を収めた。

第 7 章　日本が植民地になっていたら、どうなっていたか

If America had invaded Kyushu, I am convinced it would have been a Japanese victory. The tactics of the Special Attack Corps, or Kamikaze, as they are popularly known, had been changed. In the battle of Okinawa, and in the Philippines, they attacked American warships, and inflicted great damage.

私は、もし米軍が沖縄戦のあと九州に上陸していたら、日本が勝利していたと確信しています。その時カミカゼの戦術は、以前とは違ったものになります。特攻機は、フィリピンや沖縄戦でも、米艦艇に突入して多大な損害を与えています。

Vice Admiral Kurita Takeo. Leading a powerful battle fleet to attack the American transport ships, at the entrance to Letye gulf suddenly turned his fleet away, worried about a non existent enemy carrier force.

栗田健男中将。強力な戦艦部隊を擁してレイテ湾の米輸送船団撃滅に向かったが、レイテ湾を目前にして突入を中止、存在しない敵空母機動部隊を求め、艦隊を反転させた。

Chapter7 What life would have been like if Japan had been colonized

However in the battle of Okinawa, since the aircraft had to travel a great distance over open water, 90% of the aircraft were shot down before reaching the American fleet.

しかし沖縄戦では、特攻機は海上を長時間飛行する必要があったため、米艦艇に突入する前に、その90%が撃墜されました。

In an invasion of Kyushu, many airfields would have only been 10 minutes flight time to the American fleet. And the objective was not to attack warships, but the troop transports.

一方、九州上陸作戦の場合、飛行場から米艦艇までの飛行時間は、たいていの場合10分程度です。そして、攻撃目標は軍艦ではなく、輸送船です。

A landing ship Medium (LSM-20) after receiving a hit from a Special Attack (Kamikaze) aircraft.

特攻機が突入し、沈む揚陸艦(LSM-20)

第 7 章　日本が植民地になっていたら、どうなっていたか

Japan had over 2,000 Special Attack Corps aircraft prepared. If even 10% of them had succeeded in sinking transport ships, the US invasion of Kyushu would have failed. Then Japan could have negotiated a more advantageous peace treaty.

当時、日本軍は特攻機を 2 千機以上準備していました。その一割が輸送船への突入に成功しただけで、米国の九州上陸作戦は失敗していたでしょう。そしてその後、日本はもっと有利な条件で、講和条約の交渉ができたでしょう。

The cruelty of war
戦争とは残酷なもの

And if Americans were so kind, why fire bomb Japanese cities? Why drop two atom bombs?

それに、そもそも米国人がそんなに優しいのであれば、なぜ日本の諸都市を焼夷弾で焼き払ったりしたのでしょう？　なぜ、原爆を 2 発も落としたのでしょう？

Many American military leaders were against the use of the atom bombs. Yet they could not stop it. It was done for political reasons, to show dominance.

米国の軍事指導者の中には、原爆投下に反対していた者が大勢いました。しかし、彼らは原爆投下を阻止できませんでした。そして、米国の力を誇示するためという政治的な理由で、原爆が投下されました。

When Hitler invaded the Soviet Union in 1941, his objective was "Lebensraum" or living space for German people. But there were already Russians there. His plans for the Russian people was to Germanize 33%,

Chapter 7 What life would have been like if Japan had been colonized

exterminate 33%, and make slaves of the rest.

1941年にヒトラーはソ連に侵攻しましたが、その目的は、ドイツ国民のための"レーベンスラウム"(生存圏)を獲得することでした。しかし、そこにはロシア人が住んでいます。ヒトラーの計画は、そのうちの3割をドイツ化し、3割を絶滅させ、残りを奴隷にする、というものでした。

Stalin helped Hitler very much. In the Versailles treaty that ended WWI, Germany was forbidden to have tank forces in it's army. Stalin let German soldiers train in tank warfare secretly in Russia.

スターリンは、ヒトラーを大いに助けていました。第一次世界大戦後のヴェルサイユ条約でドイツ陸軍は戦車部隊の保有を禁じられていましたが、スターリンは、ドイツ軍がロシアで秘密裏に戦車を使って訓練することを許可しました。

The way Germany paid him back was to invade his country, and attempt to destroy Russia.

その恩義に対するドイツの返礼は、ロシア侵攻でした。

An interesting historical note. Hitler lost the war for Germany by invading Russia. But if he had treated Russians and other nationalities with decency, the Russian people would have revolted and joined Hitler against the cruelties of Stalin and Soviet Communism.

興味深い歴史上のポイントです。ロシアに侵攻して、ヒトラーは戦争に負けました。しかし、もしヒトラーが、侵攻した土地の住人であるロシア人や他の民族を丁重に扱っていたら、彼らはスターリンとソ連共産主義の残虐行為に対して叛旗をひるがえし、ヒトラー側についていたでしょう。

With his idiotic racial theories that Russians were an inferior race and

第 7 章　日本が植民地になっていたら、どうなっていたか

should be exterminated, Hitler lost the war.　There are Japanese people who say in case of invasion, we should be noble and surrender.　Really?　Japan was very lucky with the Americans who occupied Japan.　Many other Americans would have been much crueler.

　ロシア人は劣等民族であり、根絶すべきであるという、彼のバカげた人種論のせいで、ヒトラーは戦争に負けました。一方で、日本が侵略された場合、堂々と降伏すべきである、と言う日本人もいます。本当にそれが正しい選択なのでしょうか？　占領を指導したのが GHQ の米国人だったことは、日本にとってはまだ幸運でした。普通の米国人だったら、もっと残酷なことが行われていたでしょう。

Colonialism, crueler than war
戦争よりもさらに残酷な占領

　The truth is that in general, military occupations are as bad as, or worse, than the war itself.　The winning country simply plunders the defeated country.　Let me give an example using Japanese medieval civil wars.

　実際、占領というものは、戦争と同じくらいひどいか、あるいは戦争よりひどい場合があります。占領というのは戦勝国が敗戦国から略奪するということです。それを、日本の戦国時代を例にとって、見てみましょう。

　When The Ukita family of present day Okayama lost at Sekigahara, and lost their domain, if the Tokugawa had acted like normal countries, the following would have happened.

　現在の岡山県を治めていた宇喜多家が関ヶ原で負けて領地を失った時、徳川家が西洋の諸外国のような行動を取った場合、次のようなことが起こります。

Chapter7 What life would have been like if Japan had been colonized

Tokugawa soldiers would have been given 3 days to steal as they pleased from cities and towns in Okayama. They would have been free to rape women as they pleased. They could kill any citizen they wished.

岡山の街で、徳川の兵士は三日間、好きなように略奪してよいという許可が出されます。女性をレイプするのも自由なら、殺人だっておとがめなしです。

Afterwards, anything of value remaining would have been taken to the Tokugawa domains. Any remaining beautiful women would have been kidnapped. Crops would have been confiscated. The survivors in Okayama would have starved. And would have been heavily taxed by the Tokugawa.

その後、残された価値がある物、例えば美しい女性は徳川家に運ばれます。農作物は没収され、岡山では飢饉が発生します。しかも、徳川家からは重税を課せられます。

This is normal behavior for victories armies throughout history. Japanese people do not behave in this way, so it is difficult to comprehend.

人間の歴史において、これが、戦争に勝った国がとる、普遍的な行動なのです。しかし、実際には日本人はそんなことはしないので、おそらく理解しがたいことだろうと思います。

To be sure, the American occupation was not all sweetness and light. As we have seen, many people suffered. The Americans reformed Japan, without having a clue about Japanese culture or history. They made many mistakes.

確かに、戦後の米国による占領は、寛大なものというわけではありませんでした。私たちが目にしてきたように、多くの日本人が苦しみました。日本の歴史や文化をよく分かっていない米国人が日本を作りかえ、彼らは多くの間違いを犯しました。

第 7 章　日本が植民地になっていたら、どうなっていたか

In foreign policy, Japan has become a vassal state of America. Japan still does not fully control it's own airspace, particularly in the Kanto plain. But in general, historical occupations have been much worse.

その結果、日本の外交政策は、米国に従属したものになっています。日本の空も、全てが日本の領空というわけではありません。特に関東平野がそうです。それでも、歴史を振り返ると、占領というのはそれどころではない、もっと恐ろしいものなのです。

After WWII, America desired Japan as a vassal state, and so this influenced their behavior.

大東亜戦争後、米国は日本を従属国にしようとし、それが米国の行動にも影響を及ぼしました。

So would these Japanese people who preach noble surrender, in case of foreign invasion, be the first to offer their wives and children to the enemy to be killed or made into slaves?

前出のような、胸を張って降伏しよう、と説く日本人は、外国に侵略された時に、自分の妻や子供を率先して敵に差し出すのでしょうか？　殺されるか奴隷にされるのが分かっているというのに？

Another example of not fighting in the face of aggression is Hawaii. When American businessmen forcibly annexed Hawaii in 1898, the Queen decided not to resist. Today, native Hawaiians and Pacific islanders are only 10% of the population of Hawaii. They are ghosts in their own land.

侵略に遭いながらも戦わなかった例の一つに、ハワイがあります。米国のビジネスマンたちが 1898 年に、強制的にハワイを併合しましたが、この時ハワイの女王は抵抗しないことを決心しました。その結果、現在、ハワイ先住民と太平洋諸島系の住民は、ハワイの全人口の 1 割しかいません。自分たちの領土なのに、彼らはゴーストのような存在です。

Chapter7 What life would have been like if Japan had been colonized

The thing is, they did not really have the military power to resist. But it is a sad story. The American businessmen were not interested in communication or understanding. They wanted total dominance.

問題は、彼らには抵抗するだけの軍事力がなかったということです。そして、それはとても悲しい現実です。米国のビジネスマンたちは、対話や相互理解などには、全く関心がありませんでした。彼らが望むのは、完全なる支配だけです。

And no one today praises the Hawaiian people for their nobility. They are ignored.

そして現在、ハワイ人は崇高だったなどと讃える者は誰もおらず、彼らに心を寄せる者もいません。

The last Queen of Hawaii, Liliuokalani. The monarchy was abolished by America, and Hawaii was annexed into the United States.

ハワイ王国最後の国王(女王)リリウオカラニ。ハワイは米国によって王政が廃止され、最終的に米国に併合された。

第7章　日本が植民地になっていたら、どうなっていたか

Present day America is heading for Civil war
内戦が近づいている米国

Let's take another look at America today. The country is on the brink of civil war. They refuse to communicate. The fight is between the political Right and Left. But it is the Left that is bad here.

もう一度、今の米国を見てみましょう。米国は内乱の瀬戸際まできています。米国人どうしで、対話を拒否しています。政治的左派と右派の間の争いです。しかし、特にひどいのは左派の方です。

They desire to totally change society. They wish to eliminate and destroy people who think differently than them. False rape accusations, or of sexual harassment, are very common.

左派は社会を根本的に変えたいと思っています。自分と異なる考えを持つ人を排除し、消し去りたいと思っています。相手を貶めるために、虚偽のレイプ、セクハラの告発がよく起きています。

Leading Feminists declare these false accusations to be legitimate if they help destroy the power of White, heterosexual men. They have no desire to communicate, no desire to compromise.

これらを主導しているフェミニストは、有力な異性愛者の白人男性を引きずり下ろすためなら、そうした虚偽の訴えも正当だと宣言しています。彼らは対話を望んでおらず、妥協する余地はありません。

So the United States is heading to a time of mass killing. Japanese people value cooperation and compromise. Westerners, in particular Americans, see this as weakness. They prefer to force their ideas upon others.

米国は、大量殺戮の時代へ向かっています。日本人は妥協し、協力

し合うことを大切にしますが、米国人の考えでは、それは弱い人間のすることなのです。米国人は、自分の考えを他人に強制することを好みます。

And this leads to violence and wars. It does not matter if Japanese wish for peace. They will attack and destroy anyway.

そして、これは暴力、ひいては戦争につながります。日本人が平和を望んでいようが何だろうが関係ありません。とにかく、彼らは攻撃し、滅ぼすのです。

I do think the Europeans have tired of war, and really do not want it. But not Americans. They have not experienced war in their own country for 150 years. So they are dangerous.

ヨーロッパ人は、戦争にはうんざりしており、戦争をしたいという気持ちはないと思います。しかし、米国人は違います。自国での戦争というものを150年間、経験していません。だから米国人は危険なのです。

I just hope they do not launch a massive nuclear war in their chaos. Maybe not, if the nuclear weapons remain in Right wing hands.

米国が混乱に陥っても、世界に対して大規模な核戦争を起こさないことを私は願っています。核兵器が右派の手にあるうちは、そういうことは起こらないかもしれません。

Foreigners lie very easily
平気で嘘をつく外国人

Japanese people often have a too naive view of foreigners. They assume all people are good.

第7章 日本が植民地になっていたら、どうなっていたか

　日本人は、外国人に対する警戒心がなさすぎます。日本人は、人はみな善人だと仮定して考えます。

Well, Japan, if we include the Jomon era, has over 16,000 years of history.

　日本には、縄文時代を含めて、1万6千年の歴史があります。

America, since Americans willfully forget their European history, or Asian or African, has only 250 years of history. It is a nation in the making.

　一方の米国人は、アジア、ヨーロッパ、アフリカの歴史を意図的に無視するので、自分たちの250年の歴史しかありません。米国はまだ建国途上の国なのです。

But in those 16,000 years, Japan has built up a culture of cooperation and trust. Americans cannot imagine this.

　日本人は、1万6千年もの歳月をかけて、協力と信用の文化を築き上げてきました。米国人には想像もできない世界です。

I will give an example. I have written that I used to be an actor. Well, about 23 years ago, I got a major part that had the possibility to make me a star. But Americans ruined it.

　一つ例をあげます。私は前著で、俳優の仕事をしていたことを書きました。23年ほど前の話ですが、いい役をもらうことができました。ひょっとしたら、私はスターになれたかもしれません。しかし、他の米国人たちが、それを台無しにしてしまいました。

Here is the story. There was a popular weekly show on a major Japanese TV station, and one segment in the show featured an American family. There was the father played by me, the mother, and two children,

Chapter7 What life would have been like if Japan had been colonized

one son and one daughter.

　それはこういうことです。ある日本の人気テレビ番組の中に、米国人の家族が登場するコーナーができました。私は父親の役で、妻、娘、息子がいるという一家です。

Every week we presented a skit in English, that parodied some aspects of Japanese society. I remember one, I came home late from drinking. Mother and the children were sitting in the living room very worried.

　毎週、英語で日本の社会にありがちなことをパロディーにする、といった内容です。その一つを覚えています。父親（私）が酒を飲んで夜遅く帰宅すると、妻と子供たちが心配して居間にいます。

When I got home, there was lipstick on my collar. Mother got angry, but I (father) cried and apologized. So despite daughters protests, mother forgives father because he apologized so intensely.

　父親の襟元に口紅がついています。妻は激怒しますが、父親は泣いて謝ります。子供たちも怒ってますが、父親が平身低頭で謝ったので、妻は許すことにします。

This was a time of many political scandals, and many politicians were on TV apologizing. My last line in the skit was look at the camera and say, "You can get away with anything if you apologize enough!"

　すると父親はカメラに向かって、「謝れば、何をやってもいいんです」。これがこのパロディーのオチでした。当時は政治家のスキャンダルがしょっちゅうあって、よくテレビで政治家が謝罪していたのです。

Our little skit became very popular on an already popular show. It ran for some 4 months. The plan was two years, and here was the trouble. When we auditioned for the show, all four of us in that television family signed a contract that we would be resident in Japan for the next two years.

　この米国人家族の寸劇は、その人気番組の中でも、特に人気のあるコーナーになり、4カ月も続きました。本当は2年間続く予定でしたが、そこで問題が起きました。もともと、番組のオーディションの時に、その家族役の全員が、2年間は日本に在住するという契約書にサインしていました。

But families of the two children were expats, working in American corporations in Japan. After those four months, they were scheduled to return to America. They knew this from the beginning. As one of the actual mothers of the children told me directly, "Oh we lied. We just wanted the kids to have some work!".

　しかし、子供たちの実際の家族は、日本国内の米国企業で働く米国人でした。はじめから、子供たちは4カ月後に米国へ帰国する予定だったのです。2人の子供のお母さんたちは、直接私に「嘘をついてたんだけど、子供たちにちょっと仕事をしてほしかっただけなのよ」と言いました。

Until that time, the actual parents would come to the studio, be very friendly, but the whole time it was one big lie. They just wanted something for themselves. They did not care how much damage it did to other people.

　撮影の時にも、この実際の親たちがスタジオに来ていましたが、みんな非常に和気あいあいとした雰囲気でした。しかし、それは全くの作りごとでした。彼らは、自分たちが利益を得られるのであれば、他人がどれほど損害をこうむろうが、気にならないのです。

Well, of course that segment of the show was over. I don't really know if I could have been such a big star, my Japanese language ability then was not that good, and I really don't fit the TV talent type of image.

Chapter7 What life would have been like if Japan had been colonized

　当然ながら、その番組の人気コーナーは終了しました。もちろん、そのコーナーが続いていたとして、私が本当に大スターになれたかどうかは分かりません。その頃の私は、日本語はあまり上手ではなかったですし、本当はテレビタレントに向いていない人間です。

But they lied. These were elite Americans. And they took their pay and went home. On the Japanese side, there was a lot of screaming from the TV station to the talent agency, but the Americans did not care.

　でも、彼らは嘘をつきました。彼らはエリートの米国人です。彼らはギャラをもらい、国に帰りました。日本のテレビ局からタレント事務所に強い抗議がありました。しかし、その米国人たちは、まるで気にしませんでした。

Here is what should have happened, and how to deal with foreigners.

　では、こういう場合、どうすればよいのでしょう。このような外国人に対しては、どう対処すればよいのでしょうか。

They should have been sued by the talent agency. There should have been contacts to the Japanese immigration agency to prevent them from leaving Japan until compensation had been paid.

　タレント事務所が彼らを訴えるべきです。日本の入国管理局に連絡して、彼らが賠償するまで、日本から出国できないようにすればよかったのです。

If they somehow disappeared from Japan, their companies in Japan should have been sued. After all, the companies were responsible for their conduct in Japan.

　もし彼らがまんまと日本を出国してしまった場合は、日本にある彼らの会社を訴えることができるはずです。会社は、その米国人の日本での行為に対して、責任があるからです。

But Japanese people don't like legal fighting, so nothing was done. They were even paid. And those Americans have an arrogant idea that Japanese people are easy marks, easily cheated. It is likely that when they went back to America, they would boast about how easy it is to cheat Japanese people.

  しかし、日本人は法的な争いを好まないので、実際には何もしませんでした。それどころか、ギャラまで支払いました。そういう米国人たちは、日本人はお人好しでだましやすい存在である、という傲慢な考えを持っています。おそらく彼らは米国に帰って、日本人は簡単にだませるよ、と自慢していることでしょう。

For Americans, court cases are a form of cultural war
米国人にとって裁判は文化的な戦争である

  Foreigners think differently than Japanese. It is necessary to understand them, and to sometimes fight. In this case, such people will not think that lying and cheating was bad, but rather that Japanese people were naive and gullible, and thusly it is OK to cheat them.

  外国人は日本人と考え方が違います。彼らがどういう人間なのかを理解し、時には戦うことも必要です。先の例の通り、彼らは嘘をついたり、他人をだましたりすることが悪いことだとは思っていません。逆に、日本人は単純でだましやすい、だからだましてもいいと思っている、ということなのです。

  Americans in particular do not have the same cultural trust that Japanese people have. That is why there are so many lawyers in America. To Americans, legal battles are the civilized form of warfare.

  特に米国人は、日本人のような信用の文化がありません。それで、米国には弁護士の数が多いのです。米国人にとって、法廷闘争は文

Chapter7 What life would have been like if Japan had been colonized

明的な戦争です。

America is a legal culture, and a punishment culture. Since Americans come from so many nations, cultural common sense like we have in Japan, cannot work. So laws must be created, and enforced. That is why there are so many lawyers in America, and law occupies so much of the American mind.

米国は、法律の文化、罰則の文化です。米国人は様々な国からやってきた人たちなので、日本のように文化的な共通感覚がありません。そのために、法律を制定し、執行する必要があります。そんなわけで、米国にはたくさんの弁護士がいるのです。米国人の頭の中は、法律のことでいっぱいです。

Well, since people are not killed in legal battles and civilization not destroyed, this is perhaps some kind of philosophy. But I prefer the Japanese version of civilization.

確かに、法廷での争いは殺し合いではありませんし、文明が崩壊するようなこともありません。米国人の生き方は、ある種の哲学と言えるでしょう。でも、私には日本の文明の方がよいのです。

Right now as I write his, we are witnessing a extreme case of lying in America concerning the confirmation of Brett Kavanaugh to the Supreme Court.

私はこの原稿を書きながら、米国での途方もないでっち上げ事件を目の当たりにしています。ブレット・カバノー氏の最高裁判事承認に関するものです。

Mr. Kavanaugh is being nominated by President Trump for the Supreme Court. A woman has stepped forth to say he is unfit because he committed sexual misconduct at a party when he was 17, she was 15.

第 7 章　日本が植民地になっていたら、どうなっていたか

　カバノー氏はトランプ大統領から、最高裁判事に指名されました。ある女性は、15 歳の時にパーティーで当時 17 歳のカバノー氏から性的暴行を受けた、彼は最高裁判事にふさわしい人物ではない、と主張しています。

Apparently, he got drunk and groped her. He says he has no memory of the incident, she says it caused lifelong trauma.

　酒に酔ったカバノー氏が彼女の体に触った、ということらしいのですが、彼はその事件についての記憶がないと言い、彼女はその事件のせいで今も精神的外傷（トラウマ）を引きずっていると話しています。

Well, somebody is lying, but the way American politics is going, this is very serious. Frankly, even if the incident did happen as the woman accuser says, I cannot see how it is relevant today.

　どちらかが嘘をついています。しかし、現在の米国の政治において、これが非常に深刻な事件になっているのです。実のところ、その女性の主張が事実だとしても、それを今ごろになって問題にするのは妥当ではないでしょう。

He was a teenager then, and teenagers do silly and stupid things. This should not be a crime over his head for life. But the American Left thinks so. Myself, I really don't remember what I did when I was 17.

　その頃の彼はティーンエイジャーです。確かにティーンエイジャーは愚かなことをしがちです。しかしそれは、一生涯にわたって彼に背負わせ続けさせるような罪ではありません。しかし、米国の左派は、そういう重大な犯罪だと考えています。私だって、自分が 17 歳の時にしたことなど、よく覚えていません。

Mr. Kavanaugh was finally confirmed, an FBI investigation concluded that no crime had been committed. At his swearing in ceremony, a hysterical mob tried to break down the doors to the Supreme Court building. One woman could be seen on video clawing at the door with her fingers.

カバノー氏の人事案は、最終的には承認されました。FBI の調査では疑惑を裏付ける証拠は見つかりませんでした。にもかかわらず、カバノー氏の最高裁判事就任の宣誓式では、ヒステリックな群衆が最高裁の扉を壊して侵入しようとしました。ビデオには、扉をひっかいている女性の姿が映っています。

This truly shows that American culture is breaking apart, and common sense has departed. And it means a lot for people who believe that America will defend Japan in an emergency. The American military has become much less capable of any kind of military action.

こうした事象は、米国の文化が分裂状態で、共通感覚がなくなっているということを、はっきり示しています。それと同時に、日本が危機の時には米国が助けにきてくれると信じている日本人にとって、重要なことを示しています。いかなる種類の軍事行動においても、米軍の能力は大きく低下している、ということです。

And this internal turmoil in the United States is so distracting, America is failing to keep it's commitments overseas.

米国政府は国内の混乱への対処に忙殺され、海外に手が回らなくなっているのです。

There is one good thing that has resulted from Article number 9 in the present Constitution. That is that Japan did not send troops to Vietnam as America wished.

確かに、憲法9条にはよい点が一つあります。それは、米国は望んでいたのに、日本はベトナム戦争に派兵しなかったことです。

第7章　日本が植民地になっていたら、どうなっていたか

　In the new world that is shaping up with the collapse of America, Vietnam will become an important Japanese ally. It is good that Japanese troops did not fight alongside America in that country, and create bad feelings.

　米国の崩壊とともに形成されつつある新しい世界では、ベトナムは、日本の重要な同盟国になるでしょう。ですから、日本が米国と一緒になってベトナムで戦わなかったのは、よいことでした。ベトナム人に反日的な感情をもたらさずにすんだからです。

Chapter 8
Feminists destroy the US military's combat capability
フェミニストが米軍を弱体化させている

Feminists are destroying America
フェミニストが米国を崩壊させる

But I have said that America is nearing collapse. How does that affect the military and defense of Japan?

私は、近いうちに米国は崩壊すると主張してきました。それは日本の軍事、防衛にどのような影響を及ぼすでしょうか？

In my book "2nd Civil War: The Battle For America" I describe this conflict in general. But let look at what is happening to the United States military.

私の前著、『米国人が語る 日本人に隠しておけない米国の"崩壊"』でも、この内乱の概要を説明していますが、改めてここで、米国の軍隊に何が起きているのかを見てみましょう。

The greatest cause of strife and discord in America is the Feminist movement.

米国における内紛、対立の、最も大きな原因は、フェミニスト運動です。

What Feminists feel is that society contains invisible barriers to the promotion of women. They feel that these barriers must be destroyed by political force.

　フェミニストたちは、米国社会には、女性の地位向上を阻む、見えない"壁"があると感じています。そして彼女たちは、この壁を政治の力で取り壊す必要があると思っています。

They also feel that there is no biological difference between men and women. What they mean by this exactly is there is no job a woman cannot physically do.

　もう一つの彼女たちの主張は、男女の間には生物学的な違いはない、というものです。つまり、男性がやっている肉体労働は女性にもできる、ということです。

These radical Feminists are something less than 10% of American women. But almost all women who work as professors in higher education, or the mass media, are such radical Feminists. So they have more power in American society than their numbers imply.

　確かに、こういった過激なフェミニストは、米国の女性の1割もいません。しかし、大学の女性教授、マスコミで働く女性の中に、そういう過激なフェミニストが大勢いるのです。そのため彼女たちは、米国社会において、その人数以上の力を持っています。

Radical Feminists are basically White upper-class women. They come from privileged backgrounds. They went to good universities. They claim that women of the world have been oppressed by men, and male privilege for thousands of years.

　そうした過激なフェミニストは、基本的に白人の、上流クラスの女性です。彼女たちは、恵まれた環境で育っており、有名大学を出ています。彼女たちは、世の女性たちは何千年もの間、男性社会でしいたげられてきたと主張しています。

Chapter8 Feminists destroy the US military's combat capability

Their goal is to remove White heterosexual men from all positions of power in American society. They wish to replace them with women, some gay men, and some people of color.

彼女たちの目標は、米国社会における全ての権力ある立場から、異性愛者の白人男性を排除することです。その地位を、女性、ゲイの男性、有色人種に取って代えたいと考えています。

Truly, they are not promoting equality as they claim. They are promoting another form of discrimination, across a broad swath of society. Their effect on society has been huge, and very damaging, especially in the military.

実際のところ、彼女たちが言っていることとは違って、彼女たちは平等を促進してはいません。社会全体に、別の形の差別を押し広めています。彼女たちは、社会に対して非常に深刻な影響を与えています。それは特に軍隊で顕著です。

The idealism and reality of female troops
女性兵士の理想と現実

They claim to be fighting to correct this great historical wrong in human society. But actually, they are spoiled children.

彼女たちは、人間社会に残っている大きな歴史の歪みを正すために戦っているのだと主張しています。しかし実際は、彼女たちは、ただ甘やかされて育った子供にすぎません。

So in the case of the military, the Feminists say women should be able to perform in front-line combat. Until the Obama administration, there were only a few jobs in the United States Marine Corps women could not do.

第8章 フェミニストが米軍を弱体化させている

軍隊の場合でも、フェミニストは女性も前線で戦うべきだと主張します。しかし、オバマ政権以前は、米海兵隊には一部、女性の配属が認められない職種がありました。

These were referred to as Combat Arms. They were Infantry, Armor, and Artillery. When I was a Marine 44 years ago, women were also not pilots of aircraft in combat, but that seems to have changed.

戦闘職種である歩兵、戦車兵、砲兵です。44年前、私が海兵隊にいた頃は、女性が戦闘機のパイロットになることはできませんでした。しかし、今は変わったようです。

The thing is, there are very distinct muscular differences between a male and female body. Feminists argue that it does not matter. In my basic training, there was a two week infantry school. We learned the basics of how to operate as an infantry unit.

Women pilots of F-15 fighter jets.
F-15戦闘機の女性パイロット

Chapter8　Feminists destroy the US military's combat capability

　実際には、男女の筋肉には、明らかな差があります。しかしフェミニストたちは、そんなものは関係ないと主張します。私が海兵隊の基礎訓練を受けた時、2週間の歩兵訓練がありました。そこで私たちは、歩兵部隊として行動する基本を学びました。

Since I trained in California, we were out in the desert with sand and dust everywhere. And yes, it does rain in California. Marching and camping out the rain was miserable. I definitely did not want to be an infantryman. But every Marine has to train for it.

　私はカリフォルニアで訓練を行い、砂漠で砂埃にまみれました。もちろんカリフォルニアにも雨が降ります。雨の中の行軍や野営は悲惨でした。私は絶対、歩兵にはなりたくないと思いました。しかし、海兵隊はみな、この訓練を受けなければなりません。

But that was only two weeks, and after basic training I went on to other training, not infantry. For those who became professional Marine infantrymen, there is a further six-month infantry course. It is very hard: 25% of the men who enter it fail, and are sent to other jobs.

　それでも、それはわずか2週間で終わりました。そしてこの基礎訓練終了後、別の訓練を受けました。海兵隊で兵科が歩兵の場合、さらに6カ月の歩兵訓練があります。それはとても厳しく、歩兵科に入った男子の25%が落伍し、他の兵科に回されます。

The Army had long ago changed standards so that women could pass courses in combat training. Finally in 2018 The Marines changed requirements that infantry officers pass the grueling Combat Endurance Test so that women would not be disqualified by it.

　陸軍では以前から、女性も戦闘訓練に合格できるよう、基準を変更していました。そこで海兵隊も2018年になって、歩兵士官になるのに必要な厳しい戦闘耐久試験の合格要件を変更し、女性が不合

第8章 フェミニストが米軍を弱体化させている

格にならないように配慮しました。

The Marines had conducted a one year research project, which showed that all male platoons and mixed male/female platoons had very different combat test results.

海兵隊は、ある研究プロジェクトを1年にわたって実施しました。この研究で、男性のみの小隊と男女混成の小隊では、戦闘試験の結果に大きな差が出るということが分かりました。

The mixed male/female platoons performed poorly in all areas. Many more of the women suffered physical injuries than the men.

あらゆる状況において、男女混成の小隊は成績が悪く、負傷者についても、男性兵士より女性兵士の方が圧倒的に多かったのです。

Women Marines on patrol in an Afghan town.
アフガニスタンの町をパトロールする女性海兵隊員

Chapter8 Feminists destroy the US military's combat capability

Women cannot for example carry platoon equipment like machine guns or mortars, they are too heavy.

女性兵士には、小隊装備の機関銃や迫撃砲を運ぶことができません。彼女たちには重すぎるからです。

But the Obama administration forced the Marines to change standards for women, along with all the other services.

しかし、オバマ政権は海兵隊に対して、他の軍種と同じように女性兵士の採用基準を緩くするよう、圧力をかけました。

This is to promote diversity, which some people say is a good thing. Yet the Marine Corps history in combat is excellent. War brings extremely difficult situations.

一部の人たちは、これは多様性の尊重を促進するためのものなのだから、よいことである、と言います。しかし、これまでの海兵隊の戦歴は十分に素晴らしいものでしたし、実際の戦争はとても困難な状況をもたらすものです。

The thing about this diversity idea is that Leftists use a quota system. For example, if women are 50% of society, all professions should be 50% women. If Black people are 13% of society, then all professions should have 13% Black people. Anything else is prejudice is what the Left thinks. Qualifications, physical limitations, are not considered.

こうした多様性の問題でおかしいのは、左派がノルマシステムを利用しているという点です。例えば、人口の半分は女性なので、どんな職業でも50％は女性を雇用しなければならない、黒人の人口比率は13％なので、どんな職業でも13％の黒人を雇用しなければならない、そうしないのは差別だ、と左派は考えます。能力や身体的な制約などは考慮されません。

第8章　フェミニストが米軍を弱体化させている

These same political correctness rules have been applied overall in the military. In 2017 in the Pacific, the USS Fitzgerald and the USS John McCain were involved in collisions with merchant vessels, a total of 17 sailors were killed.

このようなポリティカル・コレクトネスのルールが軍隊にまで適用され、問題が起きているのです。2017年には、太平洋で米イージス駆逐艦フィッツジェラルドとコンテナ船が、米イージス駆逐艦ジョン・S・マケインとタンカーが衝突し、合わせて17人の水兵が死亡しました。

Faulty equipment and procedures were listed as the causes.

これについて海軍は、適切な機器の使用を怠るなど、乗員の訓練不足に原因があったと発表しています。

Destroyer USS Fitzgerald. Collided with a container ship off the south Izu coast on the starboard side, 7 crew members were lost.

ミサイル駆逐艦フィッツジェラルド。南伊豆町沖を航行中、フィリピン船籍のコンテナ船と衝突して右舷を破損、7名が死亡した。

Chapter8 Feminists destroy the US military's combat capability

53% of the US Navy's military aircraft cannot be flown. The Navy says there is a lack of spare parts. 10% to 15% would be considered normal.

今、米海軍機の53％は飛行できない状態です。海軍によれば、予備の部品がないとのことです。通常であれば、飛行できない航空機の比率は、10％〜15％程度が妥当なところです。

I think one great cause of these problems is the social engineering going on in the military, which is promoted by Feminists.

私は、これらの問題の大きな要因の一つは、フェミニストが促進しているソーシャル・エンジニアリング、つまり意図的な働きかけの結果だと考えています。

Destroyer USS John S. McCain. Collided with a Liberian flag tanker off Singapore, damage to the port quarter, 10 crew members were lost.

ミサイル駆逐艦ジョン・S・マケイン。シンガポール沖でリベリア船籍の石油タンカーと衝突、左舷後部を損傷し、乗員10名が死亡した。

第 8 章　フェミニストが米軍を弱体化させている

The excessive promotion of minorities
過度にマイノリティを持ち上げる社会

Northeastern University professor Suzanna Danuta Walters said men should step out of controlling positions in society. She wrote an editorial that was published on June 8 2018 in the Washington Post, "Why can't we hate all men?"

ノースイースタン大学のスザンナ・ダヌータ・ウォルターズ教授は、男性は社会的権力の座から退くべきだと述べています。彼女が書いた、2018 年 6 月 8 日付ワシントン・ポストの社説のタイトルは「なぜ私たちは全ての男を憎むことができないのか？」でした。

There is going to be much political pressure to speed the promotion of women in particular, and secondly non-white minorities in the military. I say minorities secondly because the women have much more political power, and are not really concerned with non-white minorities. They merely use them as a political tool.

軍隊において、女性、次いで非白人のマイノリティを昇進させるために、大きな政治的圧力がかけられています。ここでマイノリティを二番目にあげたのは、女性は非常に強い政治力を持っていますが、彼女たちは本当はマイノリティのことなど気に掛けていないからです。彼女たちはマイノリティを、単なる政治的な道具として利用しているだけです。

So highly qualified White non-gay men will not get promoted. The promotions will go to people not because of qualifications, but because of gender, homosexuality, or race. In the military, they are forced to attend endless lectures and seminars about "Rape Culture", Trans Genderism, and other politically correct issues. Male recruits must parade around in red high heels so that they understand women's problems. Classes

Chapter8 Feminists destroy the US military's combat capability

sponsored by Feminists teach that the US Constitution, The Declaration of Independence, and the Bible are sexist.

今や、能力のある白人男性は、ゲイでなければ昇進は困難でしょう。昇進に必要なのは能力よりも、性別、同性愛、人種です。米国の軍人は、女性が社会において失礼な扱いを受けるという意味での「レイプ文化(レイプ・カルチャー)」問題、トランスジェンダー問題、その他のポリティカル・コレクトネス的な問題に関する講義やセミナーを、強制的に受講させられています。また、男性の新兵は、こうした女性問題を理解するために、赤いハイヒールを履いて歩かされます。さらに、フェミニストが後援する授業では、米国憲法、独立宣言、聖書は、性差別主義的な存在だと教えられるのです。

A military career is difficult. You often receive orders for far away locations. In my own family, one of my young relatives, both he and his wife worked in Naval hospitals. He suddenly received orders to go on ship off the coast of South America, she got orders to go to Afghanistan. They did not have children but what to do with their pet cat?

軍隊という職業は大変な仕事です。遠く離れた異国の地に派遣されることも、よくあります。私の親戚に、夫、妻ともに海軍軍人の若い夫婦がいますが、彼らはもともと、海軍病院で勤務していました。しかし突然、夫が軍艦で南米沖に、妻はアフガニスタンに行く命令を受けました。2人に子供はいませんでしたが、彼らは猫を飼っていたので、非常に困りました。

A military life has many difficulties. So if soldiers, sailors, marines and airmen feel that they will not be fairly promoted, they will leave for civilian life.

軍隊生活では、このようなやっかいな出来事がたくさん起きます。それなのに満足に昇進もできないようであれば、軍人など辞めて民間人の職業に就こうとするでしょう。

第 8 章　フェミニストが米軍を弱体化させている

So these qualified White men will gradually stop reenlisting. Under President Obama, 197 officers were purged from the military because they did not fit in with the new culture.

そのようにして退役した有能な白人男性は、二度と軍に入隊しなくなるでしょう。実際、オバマ政権の時に左派が導入したこのような新しい文化に適応できず、197名の士官が軍から追放されています。

And then there is the issue of pregnancy.

また、妊婦の問題もあります。

In one Army brigade operating in Iraq, women were medically evacuated at three times the rate of men, and 74% of them were pregnant. On US Navy ships, 16% of the women become pregnant. They must be removed from the ship. If they are highly trained personnel in such a field as radar operator, there may not be a quick replacement person.

イラクで戦闘中の陸軍の旅団で、医学的な処置を受ける必要があって後退した兵士の比率は、女性が男性の3倍もあり、そのうちの74％は妊娠によるものでした。海軍の艦艇に乗船している女性軍人のうち、16％が妊娠するのです。妊婦は軍艦から下船しなければなりません。もしその女性がレーダー操作員のような高度な技術を有する軍人であれば、交代要員はすぐには確保できないかもしれません。

So the other radar operators must do extra duty, or an untrained person do the job. It is now becoming more easy to imagine, how Aegis equipped destroyers in 2017, whose radars can see into outer space, collided with merchant ships right in front of them.

そうなると、他のレーダー操作員が超過勤務をこなすか、練度の低い人物がその任務に就くことになります。2017年に、なぜ大気圏外の物体まで捕捉可能なレーダーを装備したイージス艦が、目の

Chapter8 Feminists destroy the US military's combat capability

前の貨物船と衝突したのか、これで理解できるでしょう。

In March of 2018, a pedestrian bridge built over a road in the state of Florida collapsed and killed six people. The company that designed and built it, Munilla Construction Management, boasted about having an all-female design team that built the bridge.

2018年3月、フロリダ州で道路に架かる歩道橋が倒壊し、6人が死亡しました。この歩道橋を設計、建築したのはムニラ・コンストラクション・マネジメントという会社で、その設計チームが全員女性であることを自慢していました。

It collapsed 5 days after being built. When it collapsed, critical support cables had not yet been installed.

A collapsed pedestrian bridge, it was built over a road bisecting the Florida International University Campus when it collapsed, 8 cars were hit, there 6 fatalities.

倒壊した歩道橋。フロリダ国際大学が道路をまたいで設置した歩道橋が崩壊、8台の車が下敷きとなり、6名が死亡した。

第8章　フェミニストが米軍を弱体化させている

　歩道橋は、建設から5日で倒壊しました。橋が倒壊した時、そこにあるべき重要な支持ケーブルは、取り付けられていませんでした。

I am not saying that a woman cannot be a design engineer. But the company involved here was very politically active in Florida politics, and championed itself as a pioneer in diversity. It seems their priority was on finding Female engineers, rather than qualified engineers. Six people died.

　私は、女性は設計技術者になれないと言っているのではありません。実はその会社は、フロリダでの政治活動に積極的で、多様性尊重の先駆者とされていました。つまり、この会社が優先したのは、有能な技術者ではなく、女性の技術者を雇用することだったようです。その結果、6人もの人が亡くなりました。

The process of creating female and minority engineers has to occur naturally. There are no invisible social barriers created by White men that Feminists imagine. Yet if standards are watered down, more accidents will occur. Systems will not be repaired and maintained properly, America will gradually decline into a non-technological society. But Feminists would rather have this than admit that the reason many women and minorities do not exist in engineering fields is because either they don't want to be there, or they didn't qualify.

　女性やマイノリティの技術者を採用するにあたって、不自然なことをすべきではありません。フェミニストが想像するような、白人男性が作った見えない社会の壁などというものはありません。採用の基準を低くしていけば、さらに多くの事故が発生するでしょう。システムの整備と修復が適切に行われなければ、米国は徐々に、技術力の劣化した社会に衰退していきます。しかしフェミニストたちは、女性やマイノリティが工学の分野に少ない理由は、彼らがその仕事にはつきたくないか、資格が得られないかのどちらかであるという事実を認めるよりも、社会が衰退する方を選ぶのです。

Chapter8 Feminists destroy the US military's combat capability

Difficulties with women in the military
女性が軍隊に入ることの問題点

Sexual relations between men and women in mixed military unit are happening, and they are a big problem.

話を元に戻すと、男女混成の軍部隊の中では今、男女間の性的な関係が大きな問題になっています。

In a military unit, relations between the ranks are closely regulated. Unlike a commercial company in the civilian world, military people do not socially associate with other people outside their rank. If you ever visit an American base, you will notice there are three kinds of clubs. There is an officers club, a non-commissioned officers club, and an enlisted men's club.

軍隊では、階級間の関係はしっかりと制限されています。つまり、一般の民間企業と違い、軍人は自分の階級と異なる層とは交流しません。米軍基地を訪問すると、三種類のクラブがあることに気づくでしょう。士官用クラブ、下士官用クラブ、兵士用クラブです。

This is because in the military, if a lower ranked person is on familiar terms with a unit commander, that person may not get nasty or dangerous assignments. This causes not only resentment among other men, but can lead to the unit becoming non-functional.

クラブが別れている理由は、例えば一兵卒と部隊長が親しい間柄になると、部隊長がその兵士を困難な任務、危険な任務から外してしまう可能性があるからです。そんなことになれば、他の兵士の間で不満が起き、部隊が正常に機能しなくなるかもしれません。

Now if we include women mixing in, we have sexual tension involved.

第 8 章　フェミニストが米軍を弱体化させている

Particularly in combat, people live in very close quarters. There is tremendous stress. Sex is a stress reliever.

そこに女性が入ってくると、今度は性的な緊張関係が生じてきます。特に戦場では、兵士たちは、非常に狭苦しいところで過ごすことになります。そこでは極度のストレスが生じます。そして、セックスはストレスの解消になるのです。

And some women will use it to gain an advantage. Even if they don't pursue this path other soldiers, marines, sailors, or airmen will imagine so.

また、セックスを利用して、自分に有利な状態を作ろうとする女性も出てきます。女性兵士にそういうつもりがなくても、相手の男性兵士がそうしようとしてしまうのです。

People are going to behave differently than they would in the civilian world. And this is something that Feminists are not going to understand.

軍隊では、人々が一般社会とは異なる行動をとります。このことを、フェミニストは理解できません。

Basically Feminists come from wealthy upper-class American families with education in elite schools. They have no concept of military life.

たいていのフェミニストは米国の上流階級の家庭に生まれ、エリート校で教育を受けています。なので、軍隊生活がどういうものなのか、全く分かっていません。

In the Marines, a 2012 poll found that 23% of Women Marines did not want to serve in the infantry. A 2014 Army poll found 92.5% of women in the Army did not want to go into combat units. This whole thing is just a Feminist fantasy. And it has caused severe to damage to the US military's ability to function.

2012 年の調査では、23％の女性海兵隊員が歩兵の職種にはつき

105

Chapter8 Feminists destroy the US military's combat capability

たくないと思っているという結果が出ました。2014年の陸軍の調査では、92.5％の女性兵士は戦闘部隊に入りたくないと思っているということが分かりました。女性を戦闘職種に、というのは、フェミニストの幻想です。そしてそれは、米軍の能力に深刻なダメージを与えているのです。

Interestingly, the wives of ballistic missile submarine crewmen are very against having women serve on those submarines. A ballistic missile submarine is a nuclear deterrent.

興味深いことに、弾道ミサイル潜水艦乗員の妻たちは、女性がその潜水艦で乗務することに強く反対しています。弾道ミサイルの潜水艦というのは核抑止力です。

Woman submarine crew members receiving a visit from President Obama.
オバマ大統領の訪問を受ける米海軍潜水艦の女性乗員たち

第8章 フェミニストが米軍を弱体化させている

They go to sea for a cruise at six months a time. They hide in the oceans, never surfacing, never revealing their position. If a women on board gets pregnant, they cannot simply return to port. It is a job of extreme isolation, and submarine sailors live in very cramped conditions.

弾道ミサイル潜水艦は半年間、海に出ています。海中に潜伏し、位置を秘匿します。女性乗員が妊娠しても、もちろん帰港などできません。さらに、潜水艦乗員は閉塞した空間で生活し、孤立した状況下で任務に就いています。

Having women around would be a very complex problem. No, women are not evil. But this is just human nature.

こうした潜水艦に女性の乗員がいると、いろいろと面倒な問題が起きます。もちろん、女性が悪いということではありませんが、人間の本質というのはそういうものです。

Yet Feminists want to change human nature. Well, the Communists tried to do that. I remember reading about efforts to teach people to become what was called "Soviet Man". This was an ideal person that put the goals of the state beyond themselves.

しかし、フェミニストたちはその人間の本質を変えようとします。そう、共産主義者たちも、同じようなことをやろうとしました。私は以前、人々を「ソ連人」化する教育についての本を読んだことがあります。「ソ連人」というのは、個を捨てて国家のために尽くす理想の人物のことです。

It never worked, and the Soviet Union today has disintegrated. The ideology of Feminism will never work either, because it goes against human nature.

しかし、それは完全な失敗でした。ソ連は崩壊しました。同じように、フェミニストのイデオロギーも絶対に失敗します。なぜなら、

人間の本質に反するものだからです。

The thing is, no country in the world can attack and invade the United States of America. No other country can destroy America. I live in Japan, and many people are reassured by the American military presence in Japan.

重要なのは、米国を攻撃し、侵略できる国はない、ということです。米国を潰滅させられる国家はありません。私は日本に住んでいて、日本人の多くが、米軍が日本に存在していることで安心しているのを感じます。

How political correctness is weakening the military
軍隊を弱体化させるポリティカル・コレクトネス

A large problem with Feminists as that they do not understand the military, or what is war. They have some image of the military as being a high-tech organization where people simply push buttons on a machine.

フェミニストたちの大きな問題は、彼女たちが戦争や軍隊の本質を理解していないということです。彼女たちは、軍隊というのは、軍人が機械のボタンを押すだけの、ハイテクな組織だというイメージを持っています。

Well, those jobs exist. But still, the ultimate soldier is an infantryman, always has been and always will be. And it is extremely physically demanding. Feminists simply refuse to understand that being in the military and on the front line is very different, much more dangerous and demanding, than being in a corporate office.

もちろん、そういう任務もあります。それでも、最も重要な職種は歩兵です。昔からそうでしたし、これからもそうです。そしてそ

第8章 フェミニストが米軍を弱体化させている

れは、肉体的に非常に過酷な職務です。フェミニストたちは、最前線の部隊というものが、企業のオフィスとは全く異なり、はるかに危険で過酷であるという現実を理解しようとしません。

Under Presidents Clinton and Obama the Feminists made great changes in the military. Under President Clinton we have coed basic training and many pregnant soldiers and sailors.

クリントン政権およびオバマ政権下で、フェミニストたちは軍隊に大きな変革をもたらしました。クリントン政権下では、男女共同基礎訓練が行われ、多くの女性兵士、水兵が妊娠しました。

With President Obama, we have women in combat arms and Trans Gender people in the military. President Obama declared that the military should reflect society.

オバマ政権下では、戦闘職種に女性が入り、トランスジェンダーも軍隊に入れるようになりました。オバマ大統領は、軍は社会を反映したものであるべきだと宣言しました。

To please women, the newest aircraft carrier, the USS Ford, has no urinals. Feminists find their existence offensive to women.

最新の航空母艦フォードには、男性用の小便器がありません。フェミニストにおもねった結果です。フェミニストたちは、小便器の存在すら不快に思っているのです。

Basic training in the military is supposed to create men out of boys. I know, I experienced Marine Corps basic training in 1974. Drill instructors were demons. Well, we were being trained to kill any enemy, we had to be tougher than them.

軍隊における基礎訓練というのは、少年を男にするのが目的です。私は1974年に海兵隊の基礎訓練を受けたので、そのことをよく知っ

Chapter8 Feminists destroy the US military's combat capability

ています。訓練教官である下士官は、まるで鬼でした。私たちは敵より強い兵士にならなければならず、どんな敵でも殺せるように訓練を受けます。

But in today's Army with coed training, a male drill instructor cannot touch a female recruit. He cannot fix her uniform if something is wrong. And he cannot yell or scream at the recruits if they make a mistake. This is because Feminists feel such actions destroy the self esteem of the recruits.

しかし、今の米陸軍の男女共同基礎訓練では、訓練教官の男性下士官は、女性新兵に触ることが禁止されています。女性兵士が着用した軍服に問題点があっても、それを正すことができません。彼女たちがミスを犯しても、訓練教官は怒鳴りつけることができません。フェミニストたちが、そんな対応をしたら新兵の自尊心を傷つけてしまうと思っているからです。

Drill instructors now act as mentors to their recruits, especially the female ones. But this does not produce people who can function in combat.

訓練教官は今や、新兵、特に女性に対する助言者のようになっています。しかし、それでは前線で戦える兵士を育てることはできません。

All of these politically correct extra duties, such as constant seminars, and being extremely worried about being accused of sexual harassment or rape have caused a great retention crisis across the military.

定期的にセミナーを受講させられたり、セクハラやレイプを告発されたりする危険性に常に神経を使わねばならないなど、ポリティカル・コレクトネスがもたらした余計なものが、軍全体に大きな歪みをもたらしています。

第 8 章　フェミニストが米軍を弱体化させている

In general, the officers and NCO's who are fighting class material, quit. They are too disgusted with this new military and it's emphasis on political correctness. The ones that stay are very organization type people. But these people will do very poorly in a combat situation.

一般に、戦闘能力の高い士官や下士官ほど、軍を辞めていきます。彼らは、こうしたポリティカル・コレクトネスを強調した、変質した軍隊を嫌悪しています。その結果、軍に残るのは、お役所的な人です。しかし、戦闘では、このような人たちは、あまり役に立ちません。

With such an influx of women, the military has to cope with a great increase of pregnant female mothers. They instruct the recruits not to have sex, but of course, being human, they do it anyway.

たくさんの女性が入隊したことで大幅に増えた妊娠問題に、軍は対処しなければなりません。軍は新兵にセックスするなと指導していますが、人間の本質なので、なくすことはできません。

Pregnant troops have to be removed from their unit. And when their job is a vital one, there is not a replacement available. Other soldiers, sailors, marines and airmen must cover for them. The overall military efficiency of the unit fails.

妊娠した女性兵士は、部隊から退かせる必要があります。しかし先述したように、その女性兵士の任務が極めて重要だった場合、交代要員はなかなかいません。その場合は他の兵士で代替し、対応しなければならず、部隊全体の能力は低下します。

Under President Obama, some 197 officers were fired. The primary reason was objecting to the concept that men and women are equal, and to transgender people serving in the military.

オバマ政権では、197人の士官がクビになりました。軍における

Chapter8 Feminists destroy the US military's combat capability

男女平等のコンセプトや、軍にトランスジェンダーの人たちを入れることに反対していた、というのが主な理由です。

Transgenderism and the military
軍隊とトランスジェンダー

Just a word on transgender people. It is now a tremendous fashion in the United States to be transgender, to be gender-fluid, or some other thing. These are people who say their body does not fit their sex identity.

ここで、トランスジェンダーについて少し説明します。現在の米国では、トランスジェンダーであること、性差流動性を有すること、その他の性差に関することが、非常に流行しています。彼らは、自分の体の性別は自己意識における性別と一致しないと考えています。

Well, if some person decides that, fine. But they do not belong in the military. The function of the military is very different than a civilian corporation. A little thing. When I was in basic training, many people in America still smoked cigarettes. Basic training was 3 months long.

そのように考える人たちがいるのは分かります。しかし、そうした人たちは軍隊には入らない方がよいでしょう。軍隊は民間企業とは全く違います。例えば、私が基礎訓練を受けていた頃は、米国にも喫煙者がたくさんいました。基礎訓練は3カ月あります。

Smokers were allowed one cigarette per week. When smoking it we had to do physical exercise. If a recruit was caught smoking outside of the allowed time, he was severely punished.

喫煙者は週に1本だけ喫煙を許されていました。しかも喫煙する場合は、体操をしなければなりませんでした。もし、新兵が許可された時間外に喫煙しているのが見つかったら、厳しく処罰されました。

第8章 フェミニストが米軍を弱体化させている

Here is why: When I joined the Marine Corps America's part in the Vietnam war was ending. So a lot of training was still centered around Vietnam and jungle warfare. Cigarette discipline was essential.

それは次のような理由からです。私が海兵隊に入ったのは、ベトナム戦争が終わる頃でした。それで、主にジャングル戦の訓練が行われました。そこでは、タバコの規則はなくてはならないものでした。

Imagine this. A 70 man infantry platoon is on patrol in the jungle. It stops for the night. At night, the jungle in Vietnam is absolutely dark. A lit cigarette can be seen for about 7 kilometers.

想像してみてください。70人の男の歩兵小隊が、ジャングルを巡察するのです。夜は露営します。ベトナムのジャングルは、夜は真っ暗です。火のついたタバコは、7キロの距離でも視認できる可能性があります。

Then the Communist troops see where the Americans are, and set up an ambush. One undisciplined Marine can kill all 70 men in his unit.

米国兵の存在に気づいた共産軍は、待ち伏せします。規律を守らぬ一人の海兵隊員のせいで、70人の同胞が全滅することになるのです。

Feminists will be the cause of future combat deaths
フェミニストが軍人たちの命を奪う

And say I men. Front line warfare is for men only. But Feminists are using political power to convince us otherwise. I remember reading about the 1991 Gulf War. An American Colonel walked from his camp to the next camp.

Chapter8 Feminists destroy the US military's combat capability

　いま私は"男"と書きました。前線での戦いは、男のみがやるものです。でもフェミニストたちが、それは間違っていると説得するために、政治的な力を利用しているのです。1991年の湾岸戦争での出来事です。ある米軍の大佐が、自分のキャンプから隣のキャンプまで歩いていきました。

He walked right up to the perimeter of the next camp without being challenged. The 3 sentries, two men and a cute young woman, were busy talking to each other, until the Colonel walked right up to them.

　誰何(すいか)されることなく、隣のキャンプの近くまで来ると、3人の哨兵、男2人と可愛い女性1人がいました。彼らは大佐が間近に来るまで、おしゃべりに夢中でした。

If the Colonel had been a terrorist, they would all be dead. It does happen. In the 2000 bombing of the USS Cole, the Captain was very worried about political correctness, and the image of a ship in Arab waters.

　その大佐がテロリストだったら、彼らは全員殺されていたでしょう。実際、そういうことが起こるのです。2000年に起きたミサイル駆逐艦コール襲撃事件では、艦長はポリティカル・コレクトネスと、アラブにおける米軍のイメージを気にかけていました。

They did not maintain proper security around the ship, and a suicide motor boat came alongside the ship, detonated, 17 sailors died, 39 were injured. A note on this incident. It was a mixed male and female crew. When the explosion happened, many of the men, instead of going to their emergency station, first checked on the safety of their girlfriends. They were very lucky that ship did not sink because of this. It was more important for these men to check on their girlfriends than save the ship.

　その駆逐艦の周辺警備が十分ではなかったため、自爆モーターボートが駆逐艦の横まで来て爆発し、17人の乗員が死亡、39人が

第8章　フェミニストが米軍を弱体化させている

負傷しました。この事件で注目すべきなのは、駆逐艦の乗員に女性が含まれていたことです。爆発が起きた時、男の水兵たちは、緊急時の自分の持ち場に行かず、真っ先にガールフレンドの安全を確認しにいきました。この爆発で、船が沈まなかったのはラッキーでした。しかし、男の水兵たちにとっては、船よりも自分のガールフレンドの方が大切だったのです。

American Feminists have targeted masculine attitudes in all areas of society. They call this "toxic masculinity". Yet the military has always had strong masculine attitudes for a reason.

米国のフェミニストたちは、米国の社会から、「男らしい」考えをなくすことを目標としています。彼女たちは、男らしさは有害であるとまで言っています。しかし、軍隊には常に、強く男らしい態

The damaged USS Cole on a transport. While at anchor in Aden harbor, the Cole was attacked by an Al Qaida suicide boat which exploded on the port side, 17 crew members were lost. A large hole was blasted into the side of the ship.

運搬船で運ばれる、損傷したミサイル駆逐艦コール。イエメンのアデン港に停泊中のコールにアルカイダの小型ボートが接近、左舷で自爆し、17名の水兵が死亡した。艦には大きな破孔が生じた。

Chapter8　Feminists destroy the US military's combat capability

度が必要なのです。

By seriously damaging America's military, the Feminists have still not succeeded in totally destroying the United States. They have seriously weakened it.

こうしてフェミニストたちは米軍に深刻なダメージを与え続けていますが、まだ米国を崩壊させるまでには至っていません。しかし、彼女たちは深刻なまでに国を弱体化させました。

If American troops ever come into combat with Russian, Chinese, or North Korean troops, they will lose badly. But this is really not their fault as realistic military training has been destroyed by Feminists.

もしも今、米軍がロシア、中国、あるいは北朝鮮の軍隊と戦えば、手ひどい目に遭うでしょう。でも、それは米国兵のせいではありません。彼らのために欠かせない軍事訓練が、フェミニストたちに潰されたせいです。

However, Japanese military planners should take into consideration this American military weakness. Of course US military officers and public affairs people will assure Japanese officials that every thing is fine.

日本の軍事計画立案者は、この米国の軍事的弱点を考慮する必要があります。もちろん、米軍の高官、広報担当官は、日本の高官に対して、我々は問題ないと保証するでしょう。

But it isn't. In 2017, the USS Fitzgerald and the USS John McCain collided with merchant vessels, the Fitzgerald off the Japanese coast, the McCain in the Singapore approaches.

しかし、それは正しくありません。先述したように2017年、米軍のミサイル駆逐艦フィッツジェラルドとジョン・S・マケインが、商船と衝突しました。フィッツジェラルドは伊豆沖で、ジョン・S・

第8章 フェミニストが米軍を弱体化させている

マケインはシンガポール付近で。

Somewhere on the net, I found a piece of information on the net that the Fitzgerald did not have watch standers on the Starboard side. This is incredible incompetence. Something is very wrong here.

ネットで私は、フィッツジェラルドの右舷には監視員がいなかったという情報を見つけました。軍は、信じられないほどの機能不全を起こしています。これは異常な状態です。

There have been women fighting in guerrilla groups around the world, but that really does not count as an organized Army. The only military that I know of that had women in frontline combat was the Israeli Army. And after the 1973 war, they gave it up.

確かに、世界のゲリラ組織の中には、戦闘に参加する女性がいます。しかしこれは、組織的な軍隊ではありません。私の知る限り、戦闘に女性兵士を投入したのはイスラエル軍だけです。しかし1973年の戦争の後、イスラエル軍はそれをやめました。

Women of the Israeli Armed Forces.

イスラエル軍の女性兵士

Chapter8 Feminists destroy the US military's combat capability

The reason was when the Egyptian Army attacked Israeli fortifications on the Bar Lev line on the Suez canal, there were Israeli women soldiers in some of the units in the fortifications.

エジプト軍が、スエズ運河ぞいに構築されたバーレブ・ライン（イスラエルの対エジプト拠点群）を攻撃した時、いくつかの陣地にイスラエル軍の女性兵士がいました。

Such units tended to surrender quickly, to save the lives of the women. This helped the Egyptian Army make a speedy advance into the Sinai. Since then, Israeli women still train for combat, but do not serve in front line units.

A section of the Israeli defenses against Egypt, the Bar Lev line.
イスラエルの対エジプト拠点群、バーレブ・ライン

第8章 フェミニストが米軍を弱体化させている

 そうした部隊では、女性兵士の命を守るために、すぐに部隊が降伏してしまいました。おかげでエジプト軍は、シナイ半島に迅速に兵を進めることができました。そしてそれ以降、イスラエル軍の女性兵士は、戦闘訓練は行うものの、最前線の部隊に配属されることはなくなりました。

And with women like Suzanna Danuta Walters in the Feminist ranks, the future of the American military is bleak.

 米国のフェミニストには、スザンナ・ダヌータ・ウォルターズ先生のような女性がおり、米軍には、暗澹たる未来が待っています。

Chapter 9
A simulation of war between Japan and a newly reunified Korea
日本と統一コリアの戦争シミュレーション

The day a unified Korea attacks Japan
統一コリアが日本に攻めてくる日

To address the need for a Japanese military, I will now present a simulated invasion of Fukuoka Japan by a unified Korea. I will show that the Japanese military is indeed quite capable, and will fight well.

日本に軍隊が必要だということを理解してもらうために、本書では南北統一コリアの福岡侵攻をシミュレートします。その中で、自衛隊の実力がどれほどのものかを示そうと思います。日本の自衛隊は極めて有能で、十分に戦える能力を備えています。

This is not anti-Korean hate speech. Japanese people, and Koreans, both in Korea and Japanese Korean residents, do not understand hate speech. Koreans and Japanese Leftists often take any criticism of Korea as hate.

なお、これは反コリアのヘイトスピーチではありません。日本人も韓国人（在日を含む）も、ヘイトスピーチが何かを理解していません。韓国人や日本の左派は、韓国を批判すると、すぐにヘイトだと騒ぎます。

No. Japan is not like America. America is a land consumed by hate. However Japanese people do not express hate like Americans do. Japanese

第9章　日本と統一コリアの戦争シミュレーション

are angry at Koreans for unjust accusations about history, which are not at all true. But this is not hate.

しかし、それは間違っています。日本は米国とは違います。米国は、確かにヘイトによって荒廃しています。しかし、日本人には、米国人のようなヘイトの感情はありません。日本人は、韓国人が歴史を捏造し、日本に犯罪国のレッテルを貼ることに対して怒っていますが、それがヘイトのはずがありません。

Hate is when a person absolutely despises even the existence of another person. America being a diverse multi-ethnic society, under great stress, it is easy for hate to develop.

ヘイトとは、ある人が別の人の存在そのものを激しく嫌悪することです。米国などは多様な民族の社会ですから、大きなストレスを抱え、ヘイトの感情が生じやすいのです。

But in my simulation, where I have a quickly unified Korea invading Japan, this is geopolitical reality. I fear that Koreans are going at unification by thinking emotionally. A fast reunification would create internal disorder that would destroy the country. Thus, in my scenario, I have a unified Korea launching a desperate invasion of Japan that they cannot win.

この、短期間で統一を成し遂げたコリアが日本を侵略する、という私のシミュレーションは、地政学的に十分あり得ることです。私は、韓国人が盲目的に統一に向かうことを非常に恐れています。性急なコリア統一は国内を混乱させ、崩壊の危険性を高めます。したがって私のシミュレーションでは、崩壊の危険性が高まって自暴自棄になった統一コリアが、日本に対して勝ち目のない侵略戦争を開始します。

And actually the Japanese government has contributed to the possibility

Chapter9 A simulation of war between Japan and a newly reunified Korea

of war between Japan and a newly unified Korea. For years, Japan has ignored the historical distortions about WWII that the South Korean Left has spread around the world, particularly on the Comfort Women issue.

そもそも日本政府は、日本と統一コリアの間で起きるであろう戦争の要因を、自ら作ってきました。日本政府は長年にわたり、韓国の左派が世界中で展開している大東亜戦争についての嘘、特に慰安婦問題に対して、適切な対応を取ってこなかったからです。

In December 2015 the Japanese government did say that it was responsible for the Comfort Woman Issue, and paid compensation. This means Japan has admitted to criminal action. However the historical Comfort Women issue was in no way abusive. The women in the Japanese run system had more rights than women in the American system in Hawaii.

US sailors lined up outside a hotel in Hawaii to visit American comfort Women.
ハワイの慰安所の前で行列する米海軍の水兵たち

第9章　日本と統一コリアの戦争シミュレーション

　2015年12月、日本政府は慰安婦問題の責任を認め、お金も払いました。これは、日本が犯罪行為を認めたということを意味します。しかし、現実の日本の慰安婦システムは、決して女性を虐待するようなものではありませんでした。日本の慰安所の女性は、ハワイにあった米国の慰安所の女性よりも、権利が守られていました。

However by not calling Korea on the historical distortions the Korean government has long engaged in, and by continuing to quietly support Korea financially for decades, the Japanese government has actually contributed to the possibility of war in the near future.

　日本政府は、こうした長年にわたって韓国政府が行ってきた歴史の歪曲にも抗議せず、そのうえ何十年もの間、韓国を経済的に支援し続けてきました。それこそが、日本と統一コリアの間で、近い将来戦争が起きる可能性を高めるものだったのです。

The government should have protested Korean actions long ago, and ceased financial aid.

　日本政府はとうの昔に、韓国の反日活動に抗議して、経済支援を中止すべきでした。

I will also show that the American military has been quite damaged by years of social justice policies, and can no longer function as well as it used to.

　さらに、米軍も、長年の社会的公正政策で大きなダメージを受け、以前のような能力を喪失しているということも示そうと思います。

Japanese people should return to their ancient roots in how to run the affairs of state. They are much superior to anything the West has created. After all, the Japanese nation state is some 2,600 years old. America, after 240 years, is self-destructing. It should be obvious which society has a future for it's citizens, and which does not.

Chapter9 A simulation of war between Japan and a newly reunified Korea

日本人は、国家の運営を昔のやり方に戻した方がよいでしょう。実際それは西洋のやり方よりも優れています。日本には 2600 年もの歴史があります。米国はたった 240 年で自滅し始めています。国民にとって未来のある国はどちらなのか。それは明らかでしょう。

A simulation. In the future, a unified Federated Korea invades Japan.

これからお話しするのは、一つのシミュレーションです。将来、統一コリア連邦が日本を侵略するに至るまでの、一つの経緯を描いたものです。

Of course, many things in the future are possible, so please look at this simulation as one possibility. (This simulation was written in the summer of 2018)

もちろん、そこに至る経緯は何種類も考えられますが、あくまで、現段階で想定可能な一つの例と捉えてください（このシミュレーションは、2018 年夏の時点で私が想定したものです）。

An American female anti Japan President
米国に誕生する反日の女性大統領

2018: In the American midterms massive fraud of electronic voting gives Democrats majority in Congress, President Trump and Vice President Pence are quickly impeached. The 2016 election is declared invalid. Clinton is too ill, an obscure politician, and Elaine Smith is appointed President.

2018 年の米国の中間選挙において、大規模な電子投票の不正操作により、民主党が米国議会で過半数を占めます。トランプ大統領、ペンス副大統領は即座に弾劾され、2016 年の大統領選挙は無効であると宣言されます。ヒラリー・クリントン氏は病気のため、無名

第9章　日本と統一コリアの戦争シミュレーション

の女性政治家エレーヌ・スミス氏が、大統領に任命されます。

Right-wing militias begin insurgency in the US.

これに対し、右派の民兵組織が、全米で反乱を始めます。

President Smith appoints left-wing Professors, mostly women, alongside commanders in all military commands down to Brigade and Regimental level. The same is done in governmental departments. These people are called "Diversity Counsellors" and have the authority to override any decision.

スミス大統領は、連隊、旅団のレベルまで、全ての軍事機構の指揮官のそばに、左派の大学教授（それも大部分が女性）を置くよう指示します。政府の部局でも、同様のことが行われます。彼らは「多様性カウンセラー」と呼ばれ、あらゆる命令を無効にする権限を有しています。

Martial law is declared. White heterosexual men heading governmental departments and military commands are massively displaced by women and minorities, and gay men. The Armed Forces suffer massive desertion.

次に、全米に戒厳令が布告されます。政府の部局や軍の部隊を指揮する異性愛の白人男性は解任され、女性、マイノリティ、ゲイに置き換えられます。その結果、軍に大量の脱走者が出るようになります。

In most of rural America, Federal Government control becomes ambiguous.

ほとんどの米国の農村部では、連邦政府による統制がとれなくなっていきます。

2019 Spring: Kim Jong Un of North Korea and President Moon Jae In

Chapter9 A simulation of war between Japan and a newly reunified Korea

of South Korea declare a unified "Federated Korea". Details of the new governmental structure are very vague.

2019年春、北朝鮮の金正恩総書記と韓国の文在寅大統領が、両国をコリア連邦として統一することを宣言します。ただ、新しい政府がどういう機構になるのか、その詳細は、はっきりしていません。

Mass demonstrations of joy occur across South Korea.

韓国全域で、歓喜のデモ行進が行われます。

2019 Summer: American President Smith declares Japan an outlaw nation due to the historical Comfort Women issue and lack of leadership positions for women.

2019年夏、米国のスミス大統領が、日本は無法国家であると宣言します。過去の慰安婦問題に対して真摯な姿勢を示さない、女性の社会進出が著しく阻害されている、というのがその理由です。

Upon the request of the Federated Korean government, all US troops are withdrawn from Korea.

コリア連邦政府の要求で、在韓米軍は韓国から完全撤退することになります。

In the US, since most women and minorities who are quickly promoted in the military and government lack professional education and experience, chaos reigns. Rural areas become increasingly semi-independent. The politically correct Feminist dominated military basically withdraws to cities while food supplies to cities become erratic. Rationing in the cities is begun. International trade collapses.

米国の軍や政府機関において急激に昇進した女性、マイノリティ、ゲイたちは、専門的な教育や経験を欠いており、混乱が増えていきます。地方の農村地域は次第に、半ば独立した状態になっていきま

す。ポリティカル・コレクトなフェミニストに支配された軍隊の多くは都市部に退去し、大都市への食料供給が不安定になります。その結果、都市部では食料の配給が始まります。国際的な貿易は崩壊します。

The reality of unified Korea, and the wave of refugees
統一コリアの実態と押し寄せるコリア難民

2019: In Federated Korea, former Southern pro-North people identify pro-Japanese and pro-American Koreans. These Koreans in leadership positions in the military, government, education and churches of the new federated government disappear into camps, and are never heard from again.

2019年、コリア連邦では、南部の親北派が、旧韓国政府、軍、教育機関、教会で指導的立場にあった親日親米の元韓国人を、新政府に密告します。彼らは収容所に連れていかれ、消息を絶ちます。

Many Koreans who fear imprisonment flee to Japan, and refuges in Japan are over one million.

投獄を恐れたコリアンが日本へ押し寄せてきます。日本のコリア難民は百万人を超えます。

In society, the disappeared people are replaced by hard-left Southerners and Northerners. In the military, all Southern Army and Navy officers are replaced. In the Army, former South Korean companies are integrated into new battalions of one South Korean, two North Korean companies. The officers of the former Southern unit are all Northerners or politically reliable left-wing Southerners.

先ほどの、姿を消した人たちが就いていた役職には、極左の元韓

Chapter 9 A simulation of war between Japan and a newly reunified Korea

国人か、元北朝鮮人が置き換わっていきます。いずれは、軍の全ての士官が置き換えられます。陸軍では、旧韓国陸軍の一個中隊と旧北朝鮮陸軍の二個中隊で新たに一個大隊が構成されます。この新しい大隊の士官は、元北朝鮮人か、親北の元韓国人のみです。

Social media is closely monitored. Any criticism of unification policy, or the government in general, results in people disappearing. Television produces many shows about the ancient glories of Korea, and how Korea has entered a new age of greatness.

ソーシャルメディアは厳しく監視されています。統一政策に対する批判が消え、旧韓国政府の要人も姿を消します。テレビでは、「輝かしい歴史と伝統の国コリアは今、偉大な時代への幕開けを迎えた」というような番組がたくさん放送されます。

Senior officers in the police force throughout the country are radical left-wing former Southerners, or Northerners. Anyone whose politics does not fit is expelled, despite seniority. A special division of police, staffed by former Northerners and far-left Southerners is created to investigate opposition in the former South to the reunification.

全国の警察幹部は極左の元韓国人、もしくは元北朝鮮人になっていきます。先任者であっても、思想的に問題のある警察官は追放されます。新設された警察の特殊部隊も、極左の元韓国人または元北朝鮮人で構成されます。その部隊の任務は、統一政策に反対する人物の調査です。

Many vocal opponents and critics simply disappear.

こうした体制を声高に批判していた、数多くの人たちが消えます。

All defectors in the former North living in the former South are arrested. Many of the prominent ones are publicly executed in various cities across the new nation. In the former South, people begin to feel uneasy about reunification.

南部に住んでいた脱北者は全員逮捕されます。著名な脱北者の多くが、新国家の各都市で公開処刑されます。南部の人々は、再統一に不安を感じ始めます。

In the Navy, all officers are Northerners, one third of ship crews are Northerners.

海軍では、士官は全て元北朝鮮人となり、乗員も三分の一が元北朝鮮人です。

In the Air Force, former Northerners and a few politically reliable Southerners are selected to fly the F-15's, F-16's and F-5's. Most Southern pilots who are not purged are regulated to obsolete Mig-21's.

空軍では、旧北朝鮮パイロットと親北の旧韓国軍パイロットが、F-15、F-16、F-5 のパイロットに選ばれます。粛清されなかった旧韓国軍のパイロットは、時代遅れのミグ 21 にしか乗れません。

A South Korean Air Force KF-16 fighter jet.

韓国空軍の KF-16 戦闘機

Chapter9 A simulation of war between Japan and a newly reunified Korea

Morale of Southerners in the new forces plummet. Northern officers struggle with the technology of former Southern ships and aircraft in both the Navy and Air force. In any case, the former Northern pilots were not very proficient with their Mig's and Sukhoi's to begin with. Pre-unification, the average yearly flying time for a North Korean Air Force pilot was about 20 hours a year. This was due to the extreme lack of fuel in North Korea.

この新しい統一軍では、旧韓国軍兵士の士気は著しく低下しています。一方、旧北朝鮮軍の士官には、旧韓国軍の軍艦・軍用機の技術を理解することが困難です。しかし元々、旧北朝鮮パイロットは、ミグやスホーイの操縦にもあまり習熟していませんでした。統一前、北朝鮮空軍のパイロットの年間飛行時間は、わずか20時間程度だったからです。北朝鮮では極端に燃料が不足していたためでした。

Despite governmental efforts to regulate the movement and actions of people, internet smart phones appear in the former North Korea, creating unrest among the population.

新政府が、人の移動や行動を管理、規制することに力を入れていたにもかかわらず、スマートフォンが北部にも普及してネットを閲覧できるようになり、人々の間に不安を引き起こします。

Internal travel restrictions are placed on all Koreans. International travel is forbidden. All foreign residents of the former South Korea are expelled, many families are broken up, as Korean spouses and children of foreigners are not allowed to leave.

やがて全てのコリアンの国内移動が規制され、海外旅行も禁止されます。南部に住む外国人は全員国外退去を命じられ、離散家族が出てきます。外国人と結婚した元韓国人の配偶者やその子供たちは、出国が禁止されているからです。

The gap in infrastructure between the two halves of the new nation is much greater than planners of the reunification imagined. To attempt to create funds for this, very heavy taxes are levied on former Southerners, causing extreme resentment. The dream of a "Great Korea" is beginning to fade.

　新国家の、南北におけるインフラのギャップは、再統一計画者の想像をはるかに超えていました。この問題を解消する資金を集めるために、南部の人たちに重税が課されます。南部の人たちは憤慨し、「大コリア」の夢から、だんだん醒めていきます。

It becomes apparent that Leftist former South Koreans, and former North Koreans, greatly underestimated the amount of civil unrest that a speedy reunification would produce. As civil unrest increases greatly throughout unified Korea, they begin to panic.

　性急な統一が社会にどのような混乱をもたらすのか。元韓国人左派と元北朝鮮側が、そのことをあまりにも過小評価していたことが明らかになっていきます。その混乱が統一コリア内に拡がり、パニックに陥り始めます。

Since open criticism is not allowed, underground networks appear in both the former Northern and Southern Koreas. Many former Northerners who are able to enter the South, look on the Southerners as weak and effete. They become arrogant, and feel that this entitles them to rob them at will. Northern sponsored crime networks increase.

　表だった政府批判は許されないので、南北双方に地下ネットワークが出現し始めます。南部に入れる北部の人たちの多くは、南部の人たちが軟弱で、退廃的に見えます。北部の人間は尊大になり、こんな連中からは略奪したっていいと感じるようになります。その結果、北部の人間による犯罪組織が増えます。

Southerners look at the Northerners as uneducated idiots, since North Korean education was primarily political propaganda. Southerners who are able to get into the North of the newly unified country feel entitled to cheat Northerners, who have no concept of business or trading.

一方、南部の人たちは、北部の人たちを見て、教養のない、愚かな者たちだと考えます。旧北朝鮮の教育は、ほとんどが政治的なプロパガンダだったからです。北部に行ける南部の人間は、ビジネス、取引の概念のない北部の人たちを見て、これは騙せると考えます。

The entire newly unified country falls into chaos, the government increasingly loses control.

この新統一国家は、こうして国全体が混乱に陥り、政府はますます支配力を失います。

The intensification of anti Japanese activity in unified Korea
激化する統一コリアの反日活動

To foster unity among Koreans, anti-Japan agitation increases greatly. The Federated Korean government sponsors a world wide anti-Japan propaganda effort. Leftists and Feminists in many European countries and the US are contacted, and provide help for exhibitions about the Comfort Women issue, and completely fabricated stories of WWII torture of Korean people by Japan.

こうしたコリア連邦の国民を団結させるため、反日扇動が急激に増えていきます。コリア連邦政府も、世界中で反日プロパガンダ活動を支援し始めます。欧州や米国の左派、フェミニストと連携し、韓国併合時代の慰安婦問題や日本人による朝鮮人拷問などの展示（全くの作り話）を支援します。

However, the effort is totally ignored by Westerners and non left-wing Americans. There is a feeling among them called "Korean Fatigue". People may not admire Imperial Japan in WWII, but they are tired of hearing about Korean victimization.

しかしこの活動は、欧州や、左派を除く米国人には相手にされません。彼らは「コリアン疲れ」と呼ばれる状態になっているからです。彼らは、第二次大戦当時の日本を称賛するつもりはないものの、こんなひどい目に遭ったんだというコリアンの話を何度も何度も聞かされて、もう辟易していました。

Also, when the former South Korean government continued to conduct anti-Japanese propaganda after the 2015 Comfort Women agreement, Many Westerners became disgusted with Korea. They began to call Korea a country that does not honor governmental agreements, a country that cannot be trusted.

また、2015年に日韓が慰安婦問題解決で合意した後も、元韓国政府が執拗に反日プロパガンダを続けたことで、多くの欧米人が韓国に呆れていました。彼らは、コリアのことを、協定を守らない国、信用できない国と呼ぶようになりました。

In Japan itself, the Japanese Left dutifully takes up the Korean propaganda. They print articles on how Japan owes Korea a debt for previous crimes, and must compensate and support the new unified Korea. Of course, these articles are based on a totally misrepresented concept of history.

日本国内では、日本の左翼が忠実にコリアのプロパガンダを繰り返します。日本は今も、コリアに対して行った過去の犯罪の責任がある、という記事を書いたり、統一コリアに賠償し、援助すべきだ、という記事を書いたりします。もちろん、これらの記事は、完全に間違った歴史に基づいています。

Chapter9 A simulation of war between Japan and a newly reunified Korea

American President Smith declares that for the time being, all military promotions to flag rank, general or admiral, are restricted to women.

米国のスミス大統領は、当分の間、全軍の将官への昇進は女性に限る、と宣言します。

2020.

2020 年。

Koreans in Japan begin massive demonstrations claiming discrimination. In the spring of 2020, Korean special forces agents disguised as Japanese Right Wingers, kill 3 resident Korean middle school girls in a demonstration.

Foreign Minister Kishida Fumio (left) and Foreign Affairs Minister Yun Byung Se. In 2015, the foreign ministries of Japan and South Korea announced an irreversible agreement on the Comfort Women problem. However, the agreement has been unilaterally destroyed by South Korea.

岸田文雄外務大臣 (左) と尹炳世外交部長官。2015 年、日本と韓国の外相は「日韓間の慰安婦問題が最終的かつ不可逆的に解決されることを確認する」と表明。しかしその合意は韓国によって一方的に破られた。

在日コリアンが大規模な反差別デモを開始します。2020年の春には、日本の右翼になりすましたコリアン特殊部隊の工作員が、反差別デモに参加していた在日コリアンの女子中学生3名を殺害します。

The Japanese media becomes more hysterical with a series of stories concerning supposed Japanese atrocities of the past and present.

日本のマスコミは、昔も今も日本はコリアンに残虐なことを行っているという捏造されたストーリーを、ますますヒステリックに報道します。

American President Smith declares a boycott of the Tokyo Olympics because of supposed Japanese crimes in WWII, and in the present against women.

米国のスミス大統領が、第二次大戦中や現在の女性に対する日本の犯罪を批判し、東京オリンピックのボイコットを宣言します。

Rioting between Japanese-Korean residents and Japanese people increases across the country.

全国各地で、在日コリアンと日本人の騒乱が多発します。

Unified Korea invades Fukuoka
統一コリアによる福岡上陸作戦

2020 Summer: Federated Korea launches a surprise landing in Fukuoka. The Federated Korean government announces that this is to protect resident Koreans in Japan. On orders from the Korean Federated government saboteurs who had been planted years ago among the Korean populace in Japan destroy road and rail bridges and tunnels to prevent the Japanese Self Defense Forces from reaching the city.

Chapter9 A simulation of war between Japan and a newly reunified Korea

　2020年夏。コリア連邦軍が福岡市に奇襲上陸を開始します。コリア連邦政府は、これは在日コリアン保護のための行動であると発表し、コリア連邦政府の指示により数年前に密入国した工作員たちが、福岡市周辺の道路や鉄道橋、トンネルを爆破します。陸上自衛隊が福岡市内に入ることを阻止するためです。

Nodong missiles are launched at Ground Self Defense bases of the 4th division in Beppu, Omura and Kitakyushu city. Most land in mountain areas outside the bases, however in all three areas there are over 100 civilian casualties. The units of the 4th division however, despite taking some casualties quickly organize to move to Fukuoka.

　多数のノドンミサイルが、別府市、大村市、北九州市にある陸上自衛隊第4師団の駐屯地に向けて発射されます。ほとんどは山地に着弾しますが、三つの市の合計で100人以上の民間人が死亡します。第4師団の部隊にも死傷者が出ますが、福岡市へ移動するため迅速に編合されます。

A few Korean amphibious vessels land the first wave, and ferries bring in more troops and armor, which land at the port. Commandos fly in by An-2 aircraft and overrun Fukuoka airport. Wherever police or Self Defense personnel are encountered, they are killed outright. In all, some 25,000 Korean troops are quickly landed.

　コリア連邦軍の第一波は数隻の強襲揚陸艦で上陸、その後輸送船が入港して兵士、戦車を降ろします。アントノフ2輸送機で特殊部隊が福岡空港に着陸、確保します。コリア連邦軍兵士に出くわした警察官、自衛官は即座に射殺されます。総勢2万5千のコリア連邦軍兵士が迅速に上陸を完了します。

Efforts to mine the Kanmon straits between Kyushu and the rest of Japan by submarine and aircraft are discovered and stopped by the Japanese Maritime and Air Defense forces. The Naval and Air Forces of

Federated Korea perform poorly. Federated Korean Air and Naval forces quickly lose control of the air and sea of the Tsushima straits.

　コリア連邦軍は九州と本州の間の関門海峡に機雷を敷設しようとしますが、海上自衛隊と航空自衛隊の潜水艦や航空機にすぐ発見され、阻止されます。コリア連邦の海空軍は苦戦し、対馬海峡の制海権、制空権はすぐに失います。

The Federated Korean surface fleet engages the Japanese fleet just east of Tsushima island. The Korean helicopter carrier (The amphibious assault ship Dokdo) and most of the surface fleet is lost.

　コリア連邦の水上艦隊が対馬沖の東方海上で日本の艦隊と交戦。コリア連邦は、ヘリ空母（独島級揚陸艦）を含む多数の水上艦艇が撃沈されます。

Two-thirds of Federated Korean submarines engaged in the Tsushima strait do not report again, and are presumed lost. The surface fleet retreats to Wonsan on the east coast, and the surviving submarines give up the effort to interdict the Tsushima strait, and form a screen off the east coast.

The Amphibious Assault Ship Dokdo.

強襲揚陸艦 独島

Chapter9 A simulation of war between Japan and a newly reunified Korea

対馬海峡に配置されたコリア連邦の潜水艦の3分の2と連絡が取れなくなり、撃沈されたと推定され、また残存水上艦艇は、朝鮮半島東部の元山港へ逃れます。残存潜水艦も対馬海峡の封鎖作戦を中止し、朝鮮半島の東海岸沖に展開します。

The Japanese 4th division of the Western Army makes heroic efforts to break through transportation barriers and ambushes by Korean saboteurs, and arrives outside Fukuoka, preventing further advance by the invaders.

自衛隊西部方面隊の第4師団は、コリアン工作員が設置した交通障壁や待ち伏せ攻撃を果敢に排除、突破し、福岡市周辺に到着、侵略軍の前進を阻止します。

The nullification of the Japanese/American alliance, the rise of Japanese patriotism
日米同盟の無効化と日本人の蜂起

American President Smith declares that since Japan is an oppressive patriarchal nation, the Japanese/American alliance is null and void. All US forces in Japan are ordered to remain on base, and not intervene.

米国のスミス大統領は、日本の女性差別は深刻だとの理由で、日米同盟の無効を宣言します。そして、在日米軍は基地に留まったまま、この戦争には介入しないよう命令されます。

Federated Korean forces in Fukuoka take Japanese school children into their positions as human shields. When parents protest, they are shot.

福岡市に上陸したコリア連邦軍は日本人の子供たちを捕らえ、自軍の陣地で人間の盾として使います。子供を助けようとした親は射殺されます。

第9章　日本と統一コリアの戦争シミュレーション

All Japanese supermarkets, food stores, and convenience stores are taken over by the Federated Korean army. The food is for their use only. Japanese civilians are faced to rely on whatever they may have at home. The Japanese citizens of Fukuoka begin to face extreme hardships.

スーパーマーケット、食料品店、コンビニは全てコリア連邦軍に押さえられてしまい、日本人は自宅に備蓄されたものしか食料がありません。福岡市民は苦境に立たされます。

Korean civilian residents, except for a few who have always been secret Communist spies, are treated the same way as Japanese civilians. The few former pro-North Korea civilians set up a new civilian government of Fukuoka. However, the command of the Federated Korean forces in Fukuoka, knowing that resupply is impossible, decide to give the military priority over civilians with food supplies.

共産主義者のスパイを除く在日コリアンは、日本人と同じように扱われます。一部の親北コリアン住民が、新しい福岡市民政府を設立します。しかし、コリア連邦軍の司令官は、補給の困難さを理解していたため、市民よりも軍人への食料配給を優先します。

So Korean residents suffer alongside the Japanese citizens.

そのため、在日コリアンも日本人と同じように苦しみます。

The Japanese government falls. Japanese young people, incensed by scenes on social media from Fukuoka, gather in Shibuya waving Hinomaru flags, and march on the Diet building in Nagatacho.

やがて、日本の内閣が倒れます。日本の若者たちは、福岡市から発信されるソーシャルメディアの映像を見て怒りを露わにし、日の丸の旗を手に渋谷に集まり、永田町まで行進します。

Japanese Leftists demand that the government cease fighting and open

Chapter9 A simulation of war between Japan and a newly reunified Korea

negotiations with the Federated Korean government. They say the abuses of Japanese citizens in Fukuoka are understandable from a historical standpoint.

　日本の左翼勢力は日本政府に対し、戦闘を中止し、コリア連邦政府と交渉を始めることを要求します。彼らは、コリア連邦軍による福岡市民に対する非人道的行為も、歴史的な視点に立てば無理からぬ面もあると主張します。

Mobs of young people break into the offices of the Japan Communist party and other left-wing political parties across the country to vandalize and burn them.

　日本人の若者は暴徒となり、全国の日本共産党や、他の左翼系政党の事務所に侵入して、破壊、焼き討ちを始めます。

The police, angered by left-wing comments about Fukuoka, do not intervene, and just prevent fires from spreading.

　しかし、あまりにも理不尽な左翼勢力の主張に反発し、こうした群衆を制止しようとしない警察官も出てきます。彼らは、さらなる大火災にならないよう、焼き討ちを阻止するだけです。

A new government is formed, promising to fight.

　新たに発足した内閣は国民に対して、戦うことを約束します。

The Japanese 8th division in Kumamoto, and the 3rd Division in Itami quickly move to reinforce the 4th division.

　自衛隊からは、熊本の第8師団と伊丹の第3師団が、即座に第4師団の支援に向かいます。

Since Japan retains complete control of the sea and air, it is felt that a Federated Korean landing on another region of Japan to be impossible.

第9章　日本と統一コリアの戦争シミュレーション

　日本は制海権と制空権を完全に確保しているので、統合幕僚監部は、コリア連邦軍による他の地域へ上陸は不可能と判断します。

Japanese forces in Kyushu begin to take back the city of Fukuoka. To lessen casualties among the children used as human shields, and other civilians in the area, they use infantry centric tactics, forgoing artillery fire and air strikes. The troops succeed in forcing back the invaders, but suffer many casualties as a result.

　九州の自衛隊が、福岡市を徐々に奪還し始めています。人間の盾にされた子供たちをはじめ、福岡市の一般市民の犠牲を少なくするために、砲爆撃は行わず、歩兵を中心とした戦闘を行います。そのため、陸上自衛隊はコリア連邦軍を徐々に押し戻してはいるものの、自衛隊員にも多数の死傷者が出ています。

Pictures of school children being used as human shields by Korean forces go viral on the web. Worldwide, anti-Korean protests occur outside embassies. The United States will not supply Japan with ammunition, but several European nations with NATO weaponry do so, along with Israel.

　コリア連邦軍によって人間の盾にされた日本の子供たちの映像が、ネットで急速に拡散していきます。世界中のコリア連邦大使館の前で抗議活動が始まります。米国は日本に弾薬の供給をしませんが、欧州の数カ国とイスラエルが、日本に軍事援助を始めます。

Facing a strong Japanese attack, the Korean forces suffer serous morale problems. This is particularly true of the former Southern troops. The Great Korea that the Leftists promised them turns out to be a lie. Former Korean troops begin to surrender to Japanese forces in groups.

　こうした日本側の激しい反撃に直面し、コリア連邦軍は深刻な士気の低下に悩まされます。旧韓国軍兵士が特にそうです。左派による「大コリア」の話は、大風呂敷にすぎませんでした。元韓国兵が

日本に集団投降を始めます。

Even though the Japanese forces are not using artillery and airstrikes, their tank/infantry teams are being used to great effect. The Federated Korean forces discover that the amount of artillery shells, tank ammunition and fuel that they managed to bring with them was woefully inadequate.

日本の自衛隊は、砲兵や飛行隊ぬきでも、歩兵と戦車のチームが大きな効果を発揮します。コリア連邦軍が何とか陸揚げした砲弾、銃弾、燃料では、全く足りないことが分かってきます。

Very quickly, the Korean tanks are immobilized, the artillery falls silent.

このため、コリア連邦軍の戦車はすぐに動けなくなり、大砲は沈黙します。

Since air and naval superiority has been lost resupply is impossible.

すでに対馬海峡の制海権、制空権は失われているので、もうコリア本土からの補給は不可能です。

All over the city, Federated Korean forces begin falling back towards the port area.

福岡市の全域から、コリア連邦軍が港湾区域に向かって後退し始めます。

American troops in Japan revolt against orders not to fight
在日米軍兵士たちの反乱

The US Marines on Okinawa revolt and kill their Diversity Counsellors. They overrun Kadena airbase and other US installations, and offer their

第9章　日本と統一コリアの戦争シミュレーション

services to the Japanese government. It is accepted. Many American Air Force personnel join the revolt, and despite sabotage by left-wing American military personnel, a large number of F-15 fighters are made ready and join Japan in patrolling over Fukuoka.

　沖縄で米軍の海兵隊が反乱を起こし、自分たちの多様性カウンセラーを殺害するという事件が発生。彼らは嘉手納基地をはじめとする沖縄の米軍施設を制圧し、日本政府に作戦参加を申し出て、日本政府が受け入れを表明します。多くの空軍要員もこの反乱に加わり、左派の米軍兵士の妨害をかいくぐって多くのF15戦闘機が準備され、航空自衛隊と共に福岡上空を哨戒します。

The Marines in Iwakuni also join the effort, and there are no sabotage problems. The Diversity Counsellors in Iwakuni seek shelter with off-base Japanese Leftists in the Hiroshima area.

　山口県岩国基地の海兵隊も、この反乱に参加します。すでに、左派軍人による妨害はありません。岩国基地から脱出した多様性カウンセラーたちは、広島の左派の日本人のところに保護を求めます。

A F-15C of the 44th Fighter Squadron taking off from Kadena airbase.
嘉手納飛行場から離陸する第44戦闘飛行隊のF-15C

Chapter9 A simulation of war between Japan and a newly reunified Korea

Russia, fearing that China would block it's access to the sea if a Federated Korea controlled by China could dominate Japan, sends it's Far East Fleet to help blockade Korea, and sends an airborne division into Japan.

ロシアも、中国の支配下にあるコリア連邦が日本を支配し、外洋への出入口を封鎖されることを恐れて、極東艦隊と空挺師団を日本に派遣し、コリア封じ込めに協力します。

The newly created Japanese Marine Corps lands at Saitozaki seaside country club. They quickly advance inland to the port area. The 1st Airborne Brigade makes a combined parachute and helicopter landing at the airport. Parachute landing teams take out Federated Korean anti-air weaponry, allowing the helicopters to land.

新しく創設された陸自の水陸機動団が、福岡市の西戸崎シーサイドカントリークラブに上陸します。彼らは迅速に港湾区域に進み、

The Amphibious Rapid Deployment Brigade of the Ground Self Defense Force, newly formed in 2018.

2018年に陸上自衛隊に新編された水陸機動団

第9章　日本と統一コリアの戦争シミュレーション

第1空挺団が落下傘部隊とヘリコプターで福岡空港を急襲します。この落下傘チームが、コリア連邦軍の対空兵器を潰し、ヘリコプターが着陸できるようにします。

Federated Korean troops have been pulled to the perimeter around Fukuoka city by the intensity of the fighting. These tactics were intentional. The Japanese Army wanted to draw Federated Korean forces out of the urban center as much as possible. This was both to deny the Federated Koreans strong defensive positions, and to reduce Japanese civilian casualties. The Japanese Marines and Airborne units overrun Federated Korean supply dumps and headquarters units.

激しい戦闘が続き、コリア連邦軍は福岡市の周辺に引っ張り出されていきました。この作戦は意図的なものでした。陸上自衛隊は、できるだけコリア連邦軍を福岡市の中心から引き離そうとしていました。市の中心部をコリア連邦軍の強固な防御陣地にさせず、一般市民の犠牲を減らすためでした。日本の水陸機動団と空挺団が、コリア連邦軍の補給拠点と司令部を制圧します。

Former South Koreans in the Federated Korean force in Fukuoka, sickened at the brutality of former North Koreans toward Japanese civilians, revolt. The Federated Korean forces in Fukuoka lose coherence and disintegrate. Japanese forces mop them up.

コリア連邦軍の元韓国兵士たちは、元北朝鮮兵士が日本の一般市民に対して残虐な行為を働くのを見て、それを嫌悪していました。こうして福岡市のコリア連邦軍は統一を欠き、総崩れになります。自衛隊が彼らを掃討します。

Having lost air superiority over the Tsushima straits, the Federated Korean Air Force makes a desperate effort. Obsolete Mig-21's provide a radar screen for the remaining Mig-29's and former South Korean Air Force planes. This is to distract the Japanese Air Force until the better planes can get close.

Chapter9 A simulation of war between Japan and a newly reunified Korea

　それでも対馬海峡の制空権を失ったコリア連邦の空軍は、必死に巻き返しをはかります。残余のミグ 29 と旧韓国空軍機のために、時代遅れのミグ 21 を、そのレーダー前衛隊として使用します。これはつまり、ミグ 21 が自衛隊機を引きつけている間に、他の戦闘機が接近するという作戦です。

The Mig-21's are virtually wiped out when this tactic is used. Since the former Southern planes are now piloted by former Northerners, and they are inexperienced with the aircraft, once combat is joined between them and the Japanese Air force, they are still decimated.

　この作戦によって、ミグ 21 はほぼ全滅します。しかし、高性能の旧韓国空軍機を操縦するのは元北朝鮮の軍人ですから、その機に慣れておらず、自衛隊機との空中戦闘によって次々と撃墜されます。

This kind of attack is used only twice, and sparks the desertion of virtually all surviving former South Korean Air Force personnel. They hide among the populace in the former South Korea.

A Mig-29 of the North Korean Air Force.
北朝鮮空軍のミグ 29 戦闘機

結局、この種の作戦は2回しか行われず、生き残った旧韓国空軍の要員たちは全員脱走、民間人の中に身を隠します。

In the short time since unification, there simply has not been time for new government to establish a secret police force to control the former South completely.

コリア連邦は、まだ統一後それほど時間が経っておらず、新政府が南部を完全に統制するための秘密警察を創る時間がありませんでした。

Centered around these deserting Air Force officers, a secret resistance group begins to establish itself in the former South.

この、脱走した空軍士官を中心に、南部に秘密のレジスタンス組織ができます。

The creation of a Free Korea army in exile, and the end of the war
亡命革命軍の創設と戦争の終結

An exile South Korean army is formed in Japan among Japanese-Korean residents and students in the country. It is led by officers who managed to escape to Japan and avoid being purged.

日本では、日本にいる韓国人と韓国人学生で構成された亡命韓国軍が創設されます。指導者は、粛清を避けて日本に逃亡した韓国軍士官たちです。

Bases in Japan are used for training, equipment and arms are provided by Japan. Since time is at a premium, armor and artillery training, specialist training such as radio operators is forgone. Japanese troops will

Chapter9 A simulation of war between Japan and a newly reunified Korea

fill in the specialist gaps with Japanese-speaking Koreans as interpreters. The force is created as a light infantry force, armed with personal rifles, mortars and machine guns. Using exiled officers and NCO's, and civilian exiles with military experience, a force of some 7,000 infantry, is raised in short time.

亡命韓国軍の訓練は、日本の自衛隊基地で行われ、その装備は日本が提供します。時間は貴重なので、装甲車両、大砲の訓練を優先し、育成に時間のかかる通信士のような職種は訓練を見合わせました。日本の自衛官とのやりとりは、日本語が堪能な韓国人が通訳します。この軍は軽歩兵部隊として編制され、小銃、機関銃、追撃砲を装備しています。亡命した韓国軍士官、下士官、軍隊経験のある民間人で、短期間のうちに7千人の歩兵部隊を立ち上げました。

2020 Winter.

2020年、冬。

A combined South Korean exile, Japanese, US Marine, and Russian force lands in Pohang in the former South Korea. They are able to quickly secure the city of Pusan. Many people in the area, chafing at the restrictions imposed by the Federated Korean government, join them. Resistance breaks out all across the former South Korea.

亡命韓国軍、自衛隊、米海兵隊とロシア部隊が連合した軍が、半島南部の浦項市に上陸します。短期間のうちに、釜山市も確保されます。その地域の多くの市民が、コリア連邦政府の抑圧的な政策にいら立っており、連合軍に加わります。そして、南部全域で反政府活動が始まります。

The Federated Korean Navy, both submarines and surface ships sortie from Wonsan. 3 Japanese Soryu class subs are lying in wait on the bottom outside the harbor. Both the surface and submarine Federated

第9章　日本と統一コリアの戦争シミュレーション

Korean ships are decimated, and the survivors return to port.

　コリア連邦海軍の水上艦艇、潜水艦が元山港から出港しますが、港の入口には、日本のそうりゅう型潜水艦が3隻、待ち構えています。その結果、出港したコリア艦艇の多くが撃沈され、生き残った数隻が、なんとか港へと戻ります。

The Federated Korean Army disintegrates. Former Northerners flee the North in whatever vehicles they can commandeer. Various military commands in the North form their own ruled areas, and the North slides into Warlordism.

　こうしてついに、コリア連邦軍が崩壊します。元北朝鮮の兵士たちは、車を奪い取って北部へ逃れます。その北部では、複数の軍司令部がそれぞれ支配地域を形成し、群雄割拠の分裂状態に陥ります。

The Kim family attempts to escape to China, but are killed.

　金一族が中国へ逃亡しようとしますが、殺されます。

The Soryu class subrine Hakuryu.

そうりゅう型潜水艦 はくりゅう

Chapter9 A simulation of war between Japan and a newly reunified Korea

In the US, right-wing forces overrun Chicago, St. Louis, and Denver. The left-wing forces put up little resistance.

米国では、右派の軍隊が、シカゴ、セントルイス、デンバーを攻略しますが、もはや左派の抵抗はほとんどありませんでした。

Chapter 10
An explanation of the simulation of war between Japan and a newly reunified Korea
日本と統一コリアの戦争シミュレーションについての解説

We should learn from the tragedy of history
歴史の悲劇に学べ

This is a simulation. It is not yet reality. A little explanation of what events I included.

前章で紹介したことは、あくまでシミュレーションです。現実ではありません。本章では、このシミュレーションの内容について、説明をしたいと思います。

Some people might think that the whole concept of a unified Korea doing something so stupid as invading Japan is an insult to Korea.

統一コリアが日本侵略のようなバカげた行為をすると考えるのは、韓国に対する侮辱だと思う人がいるかもしれません。

Not at all. I am a scholar of military history. The mistakes you find made by great leaders are many. For example, the Gallipoli campaign of 1915, was an idea of Winston Churchill's. Launched in 1915, it turned into a major disaster, costing the Allies 56,000 dead.

しかしそれは全然違います。私は戦史研究者です。歴史を学ぶと、偉大な指導者による失敗例は数多くあります。例えば、1915年のガリポリの戦いは、ウィンストン・チャーチルが立案しました。そ

Chapter10 An explanation of the simulation of war between Japan and a newly reunified Korea

れは大失敗し、連合国の戦死者は5万6千人以上でした。

The whole concept of the simulation is that a quick reunification will lead to disaster. People remember Winston Churchill for his heroic leadership of Great Britain during WWII. Only historians know the tragedy of Gallipoli.

このシミュレーションが示すのは、拙速なコリア統一は大惨事を引き起こす、ということです。人々は、ウィンストン・チャーチルを第二次世界大戦における英国の英雄的指導者と記憶しており、ガリポリの戦いの悲劇は歴史家しか知りません。

So far, in particular President Moon of South Korea, seems to be acting on emotion and not thinking rationally. This is dangerous and will probably lead to something like I have simulated here.

President Moon Jae In and President Trump.

文在寅大統領とトランプ大統領

第 10 章　日本と統一コリアの戦争シミュレーションについての解説

これまでのところ、韓国の文在寅大統領は、物事を合理的に考えるのではなく、感情に基づいて行動しているように見えます。これは危険なことであり、彼は、おそらく私がここでシミュレートしたような結果を導くことになるのではないかと思っています。

The Deep State that actually rules America
米国を裏で操るディープ・ステート

The simulation begins with a totally fraudulent mid term election in America in 2018. For a long time, American elections have been getting much worse concerning fraud, where candidates pre-chosen by the Deep State win. That is part of the continuing rancor about the 2016 election and the rise of Donald Trump to the Presidency.

このシミュレーションは、2018 年の米国中間選挙で大がかりな不正が行われたという設定で始まります。以前から米国の選挙では不正が進行しており、前出のディープ・ステート（権力の黒幕）が選んだ候補者が勝ってきました。しかし 2016 年の選挙では、彼らの意に反してトランプ氏が大統領になりました。シミュレーションにおける大規模な不正選挙は、それに対する反撃です。

Electronic voting is simply too easy to set up a predetermined result, no matter how people actually vote.

電子投票は、国民が誰に投票しようが関係なく、事前にその結果を簡単に設定できます。

Actually President Trump has managed to co-opt many elements of the Deep State and preserve his power. In the mid-term elections the Republicans lost control of Congress. Nancy Pelosi, the Speaker of the House, has announced that impeachment would be bad for the country.

However, many radical Left members of Congress say that they will push for impeachment anyway. This illustrates the chaos in the Democratic party. Actually, if impeachment of both President Trump and Vice President Pence were to succeed, the Speaker of the House is third in line of succession, so Nancy Pelosi would be President. So American policy both domestically and internationally would take a hard Left turn.

　実際のところトランプ大統領は、ディープ・ステートが望む要素を多数取り入れることで、なんとか政権を維持しています。中間選挙では、トランプ氏の共和党が議会の支配を失いましたが、民主党のナンシー・ペロシ下院議長は、大統領の弾劾は国のためにならない、と発言しました。しかし、数多くの過激な左派議員たちは、なんとかして弾劾を成功させようとしており、これは、民主党内の混乱状態をよく表しています。もし仮に、トランプ大統領とペンス副大統領の弾劾が実現すれば、下院議長は継承順位で3番目ですから、このナンシー・ペロシ氏が大統領になります。その場合、アメリカの国内・国際政策は、一気に左寄りになるでしょう。

However for this scenario I have elements of the Deep State angry at the Trump Presidency and are manipulating the vote to ensure a Democratic majority in Congress. I have no doubt that such a Congress will quickly move to impeach President Trump and Vice President Pence. This will create chaos and a guerrilla civil war inside the United States.

　このシナリオでは、ディープ・ステートの一部がトランプ政権にダメ出しをして、中間選挙の投票を操作し、民主党に米国議会の大多数を占めさせます。その米国議会がトランプ大統領とペンス副大統領を弾劾し、それが米国内に混乱と内戦を引き起こします。

Actually, as I write this elements of the Deep State are still trying create some means to destroy President Trump. Mainly, they seem to be using the Russian collusion idea, even though after two years of investigation there is no proof at all, none whatsoever.

実際、私がこの本を書いている最中も、ディープ・ステートの一部がトランプ大統領を潰す手段を準備しています。2年間調査をしても全く証拠が出てこなかったロシアとの共謀問題を、主に使おうとしているようです。

So it is entirely possible that something could be manufactured out of thin air, and used to remove President Trump from office.

それで、何かしらの犯罪行為を捏造し、それがトランプ大統領の排除に使われる可能性があります。

I think the Democratic party in such a case would fall back on identity politics and appoint a woman to the Presidency. Sometimes, powerful people make wrong decisions. By the way, Elaine Smith is a fictional person, and has no relation to any actual person.

その場合、米国の民主党はアイデンティティ政治に頼り、女性を大統領に指名すると考えられます。時には、権力者は間違った決断をすることもあるのです。なお、エレーヌ・スミスというのは架空の女性で、実在の人物とは関係ありません。

Identity politics and Feminists
アイデンティティ政治とフェミニスト

So what are identity politics? Basically, the present US Democratic party along with American Leftists have been pushing that no matter what, women and minorities must have priority in politics and society as a whole.

さて、ではアイデンティティ政治とは何でしょう？ それは米国の左派と同様、民主党が推進しているものです。何をさしおいても、抑圧されているアイデンティティ集団である女性、マイノリティが、

社会の中で、そして政治活動で優先されるべき、という考え方です。

In Japan this just not an issue. The idea that more women should be in politics is more important among foreigners than Japanese. Japan does not yet have a large minority population. There are few racially non-Japanese in the country. Resident Koreans, if encountered walking in the street, do not appear any different than any other person.

日本では、まだこの動きは大きくなっていません。外国人は、より多くの女性が政治に参加すべきであるという考えを持っていますが、日本人はそれほどでもありません。そして現在、日本にはマイノリティはほとんどいません。在日コリアンと道ですれ違っても、日本人と区別がつきません。

So, the difficulties of a multi-ethnic population that America has do not appear in Japan.

だから、米国のような多民族問題は、日本では起きていません。

I have no objection to a woman being President if qualified. However, when you make being a woman as the requirement, you lose. The country loses.

私は、ふさわしい人物であれば、女性が大統領になることにも反対はしません。しかし、女性でなければ駄目だ、と要求されても困ります。それでは国も損害をこうむります。

I think such an administration based on racial and sexual identity would then attempt to eliminate White heterosexual men from all positions of power in the United States, and replace them with women, racial and sexual minorities. This would result in mass chaos, many qualified experienced people would be replaced by people with lesser qualifications and experience.

第 10 章　日本と統一コリアの戦争シミュレーションについての解説

　そういう、人種や性的なアイデンティティを重視した政権は、米国のあらゆる権力ある立場から異性愛者の白人男性を排除し、女性や人種的、性的マイノリティに置き換えようとするでしょう。これは大規模な混乱を招き、経験のある有能な人材が、そうでない人物に取って代わられてしまいます。

This sort of thing is already being proposed by leading Feminists in the United States.

　この種の内容は、米国の指導的フェミニストたちによって、すでに提案されています。

Also Japanese people simply do not comprehend the deep hatred that is held by Feminists. They hate White men who are not gay. They also hate Japan. They are very angry that Japanese women, other than a very few individuals, do not join their movement.

　それと日本人は、こうしたフェミニストたちには激しい憎しみの感情があるということを理解していません。彼女たちは、ゲイではない白人男性を憎悪しています。また、彼女たちは日本のことも大嫌いです。彼女たちの運動に参加している日本人の女性はごく一部であるため、そのことに非常に腹を立てているのです。

They think of Japanese women as totally dominated and brainwashed by Japanese men. They simply cannot understand that the bulk of Japanese women are not interested in a movement so full of hate.

　米国のフェミニストたちは、日本人の女性は日本人の男性に完全に支配されていて、洗脳されていると考えています。彼女たちは、その憎しみに満ちたフェミニストの運動に対して、ほとんどの日本人女性は興味がない、という事実を理解できないのです。

So even if President Trump is not removed and a unified Korea invades Japan it is possible that Feminist women, with their political power, could block an American military response. It is something the Japanese military should seriously consider.

そのため、たとえトランプ大統領が失脚していなくても、統一コリアが日本に侵略した時、政治力のあるフェミニストの女性が、米国の軍事的な対応を妨害する可能性があります。日本の自衛隊は、この可能性を真剣に考えるべきです。

The race issue in America is extremely difficult. I do not think qualifications for any job or position should be lowered so that minorities or women should have those jobs. The women or minorities must make more effort to attain the positions.

米国の人種問題は非常に難しいです。私は、女性やマイノリティを優先するために、仕事や役職に必要な条件を下げるべきではないと思います。そうではなく、その仕事、その地位を得たいのなら、女性やマイノリティがもっと努力するべきなのです。

American feminists say that society has built-in prejudices so that they cannot attain those positions. They say that is why violent revolution is needed. I say that they don't study hard enough.

米国のフェミニストたちは、今の社会には根強い偏見があるために、彼女たちは上の地位につくことができないと言い、だからこそ暴力的な革命が必要であると主張しています。しかし私は、それは彼女たちに努力が足りないからだと言いたいのです。

The idea of "Diversity Counsellors" is taken straight from the Soviet Union. When the Bolsheviks revolted in 1917, they envisioned a society based on class. The situation quickly became a civil war. Many officers loyal to the Tsar attacked the new Soviet government.

「多様性カウンセラー」というアイデアは、昔のソ連がヒントになっています。1917年のボルシェビキ革命で彼らは、階級に基づいた

第 10 章　日本と統一コリアの戦争シミュレーションについての解説

社会というものを構想していました。しかし、それはすぐに内戦状態になり、ツァー（ロシア皇帝）に忠実な多くの士官が、新しくできたソビエト連邦政府を攻撃しました。

Since in the Tsarist Army, officers were aristocrats, those that joined the Soviets were distrusted because of their class. However, the Soviets badly needed their military expertise to survive the civil war.

そもそもツァーの軍では士官は貴族でしたから、ソビエトに加わった士官たちは、その階級ゆえに信用されていませんでした。しかしソビエトは、内乱を乗り切るために彼らの軍事的な能力が絶対に必要でした。

So a political officer, called a commissar, was created. They had a parallel position alongside the military officer in command of a unit. They also had the authority to countermand any order by the military officer.

そこで、政治士官、コミッサールと呼ばれるものが作られました。彼らは軍の士官とあい並ぶ立場にあり、コミッサールには軍の士官のどんな命令も撤回できる権限がありました。

This created a politically reliable officer corps, however it limited military efficiency. I think that the American Left would be quick to create such a system in civil war America. Soon after becoming President, President Obama purged some 197 officers from the military, much more than any previous President.

このシステムによって、政治的に信用できる将校団ができましたが、それは同時に軍の効率を制限するものでした。内乱状態の米国なら、左派はすぐにそんなシステムを作るでしょう。オバマ氏は大統領に就任して間もなく、197人の士官を軍から追放しましたが、それは過去のどの大統領よりも多いものでした。

Chapter10 An explanation of the simulation of war between Japan and a newly reunified Korea

South Koreans do not know history or reality
歴史の真実を知らない韓国人

I think that in present day South Korea too many people have a fantasy-based idea of history and present day reality. Since the Kim Dae Jung Presidency of South Korea from 1998 to 2003, a very virulent form of anti-Japanese education has been promoted in schools. Also the realities of the 1950 to 1953 Korean war have been altered.

今の韓国には、歴史や、こんにちの現実をファンタジーに基づいて考えている人が多過ぎます。1998年から2003年までの金大中大統領の時代以降、韓国の学校では激しい反日教育が進められています。また、朝鮮戦争（1950〜1953）の現実も変えられています。

The goal is to give South Koreans a positive view of North Korea, and down play the brutalities of the North Koreans in the war. As much as possible, Japan is to be blamed for anything bad that happened.

その目的は、北朝鮮を肯定的に捉える考えを韓国人に植えつけ、朝鮮戦争での北朝鮮軍による残虐行為をなかったことのようにするためです。彼らは、何かひどい事件が起きると、とにかく日本のせいにします。

I have seen videos in Japanese of such education in primary schools in Korea. Kim Jong Il is portrayed as a good man who is working hard for Korean reunification. In the interview, the teachers say it is their responsibility to give a positive view of North Korea.

韓国の小学校でそういう反日教育が行われているのを、ビデオで見たことがあります。その一方で、北朝鮮の金正日総書記は、統一のために一生懸命努力している善人のように教えていました。インタビューで先生たちは、北朝鮮について肯定的な視点で見ることを

第 10 章　日本と統一コリアの戦争シミュレーションについての解説

生徒に教えることが、自分たちの責任であると話していました。

This is despite the fact that during the annexation period to Japan the Japanese government completely modernized the country, giving it a sanitation and health system, education for all including women, revived the native Hangul writing system, created a financial and banking system, reformed agriculture and fisheries, created a forestry bureau, the accomplishments of Japan in Korea are manifold.

しかし、併合時代の日本は朝鮮を近代化し、公衆衛生と医療制度の確立、女性を含む全国民への教育の普及、ハングル文字の復活、金融、銀行制度の構築、農業漁業を改革した農林局の設置など、その業績は数多くあるのです。

For example, at the time of annexation, literacy in Yi Dynasty Korea was only about 6%. And they did not use the Hangul script. The creation of Hangul was sponsored by King Sejong in around 1444. Since it is an alphabet, unlike the ideographs of Chinese, it's use spread among the common people.

例えば、日韓併合時には、李氏朝鮮の識字率はわずか 6％でした。また、ハングル文字も使用していませんでした。ハングルは 1444 年頃に世宗大王によって創製されました。漢字と違い、アルファベットのように単純なので、平民の間で普及しました。

But aristocrats resented Hangul, seeing as an infringement of the power to control information. King Yeonsangun who reigned from 1494 to 1506 banned the use of Hangul.

しかし貴族たちは、ハングル文字を、情報を支配する自分たちの権限を侵すものだと考え、いまいましく思っていました。そして、1494 年から 1506 年まで君臨した燕山君王によって、ハングル文字の使用は禁止されました。

Fukuzawa Yukichi discovered the Hangul alphabet, and after annexation occurred, it was reintroduced to Korea. From then on, it was used in Korean school textbooks.

福澤諭吉がハングル文字に着目し、韓国併合時代に、朝鮮に再び導入されました。当時の朝鮮の学校教科書には、ハングル文字が使われています。

Koreans have always had jealousy after the war over this issue of annexation, and this jealousy has deformed their character.

戦後、コリアンたちは併合されたことで日本を逆恨みしてきましたが、それが彼らの性格を歪めました。

The Kim family and the power brokers of North Korea
金一族と北朝鮮の権力者たち

I do not doubt the intelligence and ruthlessness of Kim Jong Un. All of the Kim's, Kim Il Sung the grandfather, Kim Jong Il the son, and now Kim Jong Un the grandson would not have been able to hold on to power if they were not intelligent and ruthless.

現在の金正恩総書記は、知性だけでなく冷酷さも兼ね備えた人物であることは、間違いありません。祖父の金日成、父の金正日もそうですが、知性と冷酷さがなければ、あれだけの権力を維持できなかったでしょう。

However, by Kim Jong Un agreeing to hold a historic meeting with American President Trump, it seems that North Korea has finally reached a point of desperation. And this is dangerous.

金正恩総書記は、トランプ大統領との歴史的会談に応じましたが、

第 10 章　日本と統一コリアの戦争シミュレーションについての解説

北朝鮮はかなり追い詰められているようです。そして、これは危険な状態です。

Kim Il Sung at the time of the Korean war.
朝鮮戦争当時の金日成

In the South, President Moon Jae In is not of the same caliber of toughness. What would be ideal in South Korea now would be a strong and intelligent leader like Park Chung Hee. Very unfortunately, that is not the case.

韓国の文在寅大統領には、タフな精神力はありません。現在の韓国にとっての理想的なリーダーは、かつての朴正煕大統領のような、強くて知的な人物です。残念ながら、今の大統領はそうではありません。

After a quick unification, the North would be very worried about preserving the power of the Kim family, and reducing the temptations of Southern consumer society upon Northerners.

性急に南北統一を成し遂げた後、北の権力者たちは、金一族の権力を維持することと、北部の国民を南部の消費社会の誘惑にさらされないようにすることに、大変気をつかいます。

Northerners would move quickly to eliminate any potential political

Chapter10 An explanation of the simulation of war between Japan and a newly reunified Korea

opposition in the South before they could organize. They would kill many, and many Koreans would flee to Japan.

そのため、北の権力者たちは迅速に行動し、潜在的敵対者が組織的な行動をとる前に抹殺するでしょう。人々は大勢殺害され、多くのコリアンが日本に脱出してきます。

Before the Korean war, several hundred-thousand Leftist Koreans escaped bloody purges in South Korea, and these are the source of Korean residents in Japan today.

実際、朝鮮戦争の前には、数十万人の左派の韓国人が、韓国での血の粛清を逃れて日本に密航し、在日韓国人となりました。

Written blood oaths by Korean youth volunteers,
"Please accept me I promise to fight to the death!"

朝鮮人青年による血書志願書「一死報恩 ゼヒ私ヲ志願兵ニ 取ッテ下サイ」

第10章　日本と統一コリアの戦争シミュレーションについての解説

Some of my Western readers might be surprised at this. Koreans often express extreme hatred of Japan. So why flee to Japan in a crises? The fact is Koreans are envious of Japan's cultural, political, and military achievements.

ここで、西洋人の読者は驚くかもしれません。韓国人はいつも日本に憎しみの感情をぶつけているのに、どうしてその日本に逃げるのだろうか、と。実際は、韓国人は日本の文化や政治、それに戦争における日本の偉業を、うらやましく思っているのです。

During World War II, Koreans were overwhelmingly patriotic Japanese citizens. After the war, they suddenly claimed themselves victims of Japan. In post-war Japan, Koreans ran riot throughout Japan, and claimed many locations of prime real estate as their own.

大東亜戦争の時、当時の朝鮮半島出身者は、愛国心の強い日本国民ばかりでした。しかし戦後、突然彼らは、自分たちは日本の犠牲者だと主張し始めました。敗戦後の日本で朝鮮人が暴動を起こし、街の多くの一等地を自分たちのものだと主張しました。

The Japanese police force had been disbanded, the Allied occupation force had no idea who Koreans were, so they succeeded in making many fraudulent acquisitions.

日本の警察は弱体化させられており、進駐軍は朝鮮人のことをよく知らず、彼らはまんまと不正に土地を手に入れることに成功しました。

The lies and exaggerations of the anti Japan movement
嘘と誇張の反日活動

When Koreans travel overseas, they often pretend to be Japanese. America is full of Korean massage parlors that offer sexual services -- they are all

Korean, but use Japanese names and many pretend to have Japanese girls.

韓国人は海外で、よく日本人になりすまします。米国には性的なサービスを提供する韓国人経営のマッサージパーラーがたくさんありますが、そうした店の女性たちは、みんな韓国人なのに日本名を名乗り、日本人女性になりすましています。

I have seen on YouTube a Korean television variety show where Koreans boast how when caught overseas for doing something bad by local authorities, they claim to be Japanese.

私が動画サイトのユーチューブで見た韓国のテレビのバラエティーショーでは、ある韓国人が、海外で悪いことをするときは、俺は日本人だと主張すればいいんだよ、と得意げに話していました。

Leftist elements in South Korea have always promoted hatred of Japan, based on lies and exaggeration. The Comfort Women issue is an example of this. Hard Left South Korean organizations erect Comfort Women statues around the world in the name of human rights. It is actually anti-Japanese activity.

昔から韓国の左派は、嘘と誇張で、日本に対する憎しみを増長させてきました。慰安婦問題などは、そのよい例です。韓国の極左団体が、人権の名のもとに世界中に慰安婦記念碑を建てていますが、実際のところは反日が目的の活動です。

The Comfort women system did exist, but it was no where near the hell that Koreans claim it to be. Women in the Japanese run system had more rights than American women in the American Comfort Women system in Hawaii.

確かに、戦地に慰安所は存在していましたが、韓国人の言う、地獄のようなところとは全く違います。先にも述べたように、日本の慰安所で働く女性には、ハワイの慰安所で働く米国の慰安婦よりも、

第10章　日本と統一コリアの戦争シミュレーションについての解説

多くの権利がありました。

The people who are planning for this quick reunification seem to have a very naive rosy kind of view. They have been teaching false history for so long, they believe it themselves.

性急な南北統一を計画している人たちは、あまりにも楽観的すぎるように思えます。彼らは長い間、偽りの歴史を教えてきたために、自分たち自身もそれを信じています。

For example, they want to teach Korean children that Koreans would not harm Koreans. Thusly for a time the history of the Korean war was changed in text books saying that it was fought against Japan.

例えば、彼らは韓国の子供たちに、「コリアンはコリアンに悪いことはしない」と教えたいと考えています。

All atrocities and mass killings were done by the Japanese. Complete fantasy. I remember Dr. Han, one of my Korean students of English when I lived in Korea 38 years ago. When the UN forces, (primarily American, also British and Turkish) pushed north towards the Yalu river border with China, they were met by Chinese armies which then made great advances southward.

一方で、あらゆる残虐行為、大虐殺は、日本人がやったことになっています。私は38年前に韓国に住んでいて、英語教師をしていましたが、私の教え子だったハン博士のことを思い出します。国連軍（主力は米国、英国、トルコ）は、中国との国境である鴨緑江に向かって北進しましたが、中国軍と衝突し、南に押し戻されました。

Many Korean civilians, after five years of North Korean rule, took this opportunity to flee south. Dr. Han's family was one of these. His mother stayed behind at the family home in the North, and he never saw her again. With his brothers, sisters and father, he ran south.

5年間北朝鮮に統治されていた多くのコリアンが、この時、南に逃げました。ハン博士の家族もそうでした。北の実家には母親が残りましたが、彼は二度と母に会うことはできませんでした。彼は父親、兄弟とともに、南へ逃げました。

He remembers seeing civilians on the roadside the North Korean army had caught escaping south. They had been crucified, and then killed. On their bodies, signs were put up, "Do not go south!"

彼は北朝鮮軍に捕らえられた一般市民を見たことを覚えていました。彼らは道の傍らで吊されていました。死体には「南へ行くな！」と書かれた板がかけられていました。

The Korean war and the escapees from the North
朝鮮戦争と脱北者

The Korean war was very brutal, on both sides. In histories of the war, whenever the North Korean army took American prisoners, they usually killed them on the spot. Many Americans were saved to become POW's by Chinese troops who happened to come by. The Chinese would stop such arbitrary executions.

朝鮮戦争は、双方にとって非常に残酷なものでした。北朝鮮軍は投降した米国兵を、たいていその場で殺しました。助かったのは、中国軍の捕虜となった米国兵でした。人民解放軍は、そのような勝手な処刑をさせなかったのでしょう。

South Korean forces were not shy about shooting anyone suspected of having Communist sympathies. Recently, censorship in South Korea is increasing. Opinions opposed to unification with the North are not allowed on the media.

第 10 章　日本と統一コリアの戦争シミュレーションについての解説

韓国軍も、共産主義に共感しているとおぼしき人物を躊躇なく殺しました。最近では、韓国でも検閲が強くなってきており、マスコミが北朝鮮との統一に批判的な主張をすることは、困難になっています。

YouTube is being censored. Far Left groups are holding public rallies calling defectors from the North "Scum". They have put up posters with the names of photos of individual defectors, saying that they are searching for these people.

ユーチューブも検閲されています。極左のグループは公の集会で脱北者を「クズ」と呼び、彼ら脱北者の顔写真と名前が入った尋ね人のポスターを掲示しています。

The reasons for searching for them cannot be benign. The government itself is telling defectors to not speak badly about the North. In recent talks between Northern and Southern officials, the Southern Unification Ministry banned a Chosun Ilbo journalist from covering the talks, because he was a defector from the North.

もちろん、彼らが脱北者を探すのは、善意によるものではありません。政府も脱北者に、北朝鮮の批判はするなと口止めしています。最近行われた南北閣僚級会談では、韓国統一部は元脱北者の朝鮮日報記者を取材団から外しました。

A climate of fear is being created in South Korea. The left-wing people who are pushing this are dangerous. They are living in a fantasy, that cannot be realized. And are now beginning a rule of terror to enforce their view upon society.

韓国では、粛清の恐怖を煽る風潮が作られています。これを推進している左派の人たちは危険な存在です。彼らは幻想の世界に生きており、彼らが抱く幻想が実現することはありません。しかし、自

Chapter10 An explanation of the simulation of war between Japan and a newly reunified Korea

分たちの考え方を社会に強制するために、それを批判する者は粛清されるという雰囲気を作り始めているのです。

So it is no exaggeration to say that in the future of a unified Korea, in order to distract people from the turmoil of a fast reunification that leaders will use hatred of Japan to distract people from the problems and the left-wing terror that would occur.

そして将来、統一コリアで起きる混乱、左派による粛清から国民の目を逸らすために、指導者たちは反日を利用するでしょう。これは当然起こり得ることです。

I think that this type of philosophy would trap leaders of a unified Korea into war against Japan, which with a Korean society in chaos, it is certain that the Koreans would lose.

この反日の原理が、やがて統一コリアの指導者たちに、日本との戦争を決断させることになります。しかしコリア社会が混乱した状況では、日本に勝つことはできないでしょう。

While many Japanese would indeed die, and be troubled, the most miserable victims of such a war would be the Korean people. Japan would survive as a nation, while Korea would not.

確かに多くの日本人が死に、日本国内は混乱するでしょう。しかし、最も悲惨な目に遭うのは、コリアの国民です。日本という国は存続しますが、コリアは消えてなくなります。

In America, such a radical feminist-led left-wing government would bring on civil war, and they would quickly lose control of the countryside.

米国では、過激な左派フェミニスト政権が内乱を招きますが、すぐに地方での統治能力を失います。

In Korea, there would at first be joy at the reunification, but gradually people in the former South would become irked at increasing restrictions. The new government would move quickly to quash any possible dissent. Many would flee to Japan, and I think the number of one million Korean refugees is conservative.

コリアでは、統一を成し遂げた当初は国中が歓喜に沸き立ちますが、南部の人たちは、どんどん自由が制限されていくことに反発しはじめます。新政府は、こうした不満分子の芽を、すぐに摘み取るでしょう。多くの人が日本へ逃げようとします。その数は、おそらく百万をはるかに超える数になるでしょう。

Could the internet destroy North Korea?
インターネットが北朝鮮を滅ぼす？

Also, people in the former North would have increased contact with people in the South. This would lead to consumer goods, and interesting technology getting into the former North. This could definitely create unrest among former Northerners.

一方、北部の人たちは南部の人たちとの接触が増え、それによって消費財や興味深いテクノロジーが北部に浸透していきます。それらは間違いなく、北部の人たちに混乱をもたらすことになるでしょう。

There are signs that the present North Korean government is preparing for this. I have read about an increase in propaganda how North Korea is the best country in the world, and not to be deceived by other nations.

現在、北朝鮮がそうした事態に備えようとしているかのような兆候があります。北朝鮮が世界で最も優れた国であり、他の国の嘘にだまされてはならないというプロパガンダが増えている、という情報があるのです。

Chapter10　An explanation of the simulation of war between Japan and a newly reunified Korea

This appears to be an effort to appeal to the people to not be deceived by the consumer luxuries of other nations, if they may encounter them.

それによっておそらく、他国のぜいたく品に惑わされないように、と人々に注意喚起しているのでしょう。

It won't work. Some years ago, a joint manufacturing zone was established in Kaesong, just north of the DMZ. The management was South Korean, the workers were North Korean. Every day, the management would journey across the DMZ.

しかし、そんなことをしても無駄です。何年か前に、非武装地帯のすぐ北にある開城市に南北共同の工業団地が造られました。経営者は韓国人、労働者は北朝鮮人であり、毎日、韓国の経営陣は非武装地帯を渡りました。

The Northern workers were paid about $100 US a month, but about 70% was deducted by the North Korean government. So as a reward to the workers, the Southern managers began to give them Choco Pie, a popular South Korean pastry.

北の労働者たちには、月に約100米ドルの賃金が支払われましたが、北朝鮮政府はその7割もの上前をはねました。労働者たちは、賃金の他にも、もらっていたものがありました。人気の韓国のお菓子、チョコパイです。

A huge black market smuggling operation appeared for Choco Pie. Since smuggling goods from the South brings death in North Korea, it was very dangerous. However, the Choco Pies could not be stopped, and the snacks began being used as currency.

すると次に、チョコパイの巨大なヤミ市場が現れました。北朝鮮では韓国から密輸をすると死刑になるので、それは非常に危険な行為でした。しかし政府はそれを止めることができず、そのうちチョ

第 10 章 日本と統一コリアの戦争シミュレーションについての解説

コパイが通貨として使われ始めました。

One would think that in a dictatorship, such things could be controlled, but they could not. The North Korean government ended up making a copy of the confectionary.

独裁国なんだからそんなものはコントロールできるだろうと思うかもしれませんが、できませんでした。結局、北朝鮮政府が、そのお菓子をまねて作ることになりました。

This also shows us that the North Korean people may be getting tired of years of austerity, which would terrify the North Korean government, and force them into desperate measures such as quick reunification.

このことからも、北朝鮮の国民は長年の耐乏生活に嫌気がさしているらしいことが分かります。韓国との格差の存在に北朝鮮政府は不安をつのらせ、それが、再統一のような窮余の策を急がせる圧力となっているのです。

Also, I don't think that the North Korean leadership truly understands the internet. Somewhere I remember reading that there are only about 100 international internet capable computer terminals in North Korea. When viewed, they could only be viewed by 3 people at a time.

また、北朝鮮の指導者たちは、インターネットというものを理解していません。北朝鮮にはインターネットに接続できるコンピュータ端末が100台くらいしかない、という記事を読んだことがあります。しかも、一度に3人しか閲覧できないということでした。

This would ensure that no unapproved material was seen, and these people would be those highly trusted by the regime.

確かにそこまで徹底すれば、見られて困るものを見られる危険性はなくなります。それに、それらの端末を操作できるのは、政府の

Chapter10 An explanation of the simulation of war between Japan and a newly reunified Korea

信頼が特に厚い人たちでしょうから。

When visitors come to North Korea today, their cell phone use is monitored while in the country. But with a quick reunification, it would be impossible to control the large numbers of Southerners entering the North.

北朝鮮を訪れる観光客は、北朝鮮にいる間、携帯電話の使用が管理されます。しかし南北が統一されたら、南部から多くの人が北部を訪れるようになり、彼らがそれを完全に管理するのは、おそらく不可能になるでしょう。

Recently President Moon of the South has proposed a rail link from the South to the North and to China beyond. Having trains run if people don't ride them makes no sense. And it will be impossible to monitor every smart phone from every person entering the North.

最近、文在寅大統領が、韓国から北朝鮮を経由して中国に鉄道を繋げることを提案しています。鉄道を通したら、人を乗せないわけにはいきません。その場合も、北朝鮮に入る全ての人のスマートフォンを管理するのは不可能でしょう。

The effect will be electrifying. There is already a very vibrant Korean language internet culture in the South. Exposing Northerners to this could destabilize the whole country in a matter of weeks, and events would slip out of control.

インターネットによる影響は、北朝鮮にとって衝撃的なものになるでしょう。現在、韓国語によるインターネット文化は非常に活気があります。北朝鮮にそんなインターネット文化が入り込んだら、数週間で国中が不安定になり、統制が効かなくなるでしょう。

South Korea today is one of the most wired countries in the world, with a tremendous internet presence. This simply cannot be eliminated or controlled. And in a newly unified country, the government would not be able to prevent former Northern citizens from experiencing the internet.

　韓国は、インターネットが最も普及している国の一つです。これを簡単に排除したり、統制したりすることは不可能です。同時に、南北が統一国家になれば、北部の人々がインターネットにアクセスすることを、政府はもう阻止できなくなるでしょう。

This kind of thing could panic leaders into military adventures, even if they know they will not work well.

　そういう状況になった場合、冷静さを欠いた指導者は、たとえ失敗する可能性が高くとも、軍事的な冒険に出るという選択をするかもしれないのです。

Moon Jae In, the most dangerous President
文在寅という最も危険な大統領

President Moon Jae In of South Korea is the most dangerous man in all of this. In my opinion more than Kim Jong Un, he is pushing for fast reunification. I have read that he believed he would be awarded the Nobel Peace Prize for his efforts towards the North. But many previous Southern leaders have made overtures to the North, with little concrete result.

　以上のように想定される状況において、最も危険な人物は文在寅大統領です。彼は、金正恩総書記より統一を急いでいるように感じます。文在寅大統領は、南北統一を果たすことができればノーベル平和賞を受賞できると信じている、という記事を読んだことがあります。しかし、これまで多くの韓国の指導者が北と交渉してきましたが、具体的な成果はほとんどありませんでした。

Simply by beginning talks will not bring the Nobel Peace Prize. But this shows that President Moon is very vain. He will try to force the South to accommodate the North for his ambition. As a national leader he should have more humility. He should think of beginning a process, that will take 30 to 50 years, and that he will not live to finish.

単に南北会談を行っただけではノーベル平和賞は得られませんが、このノーベル平和賞を望んでいるという話は、文在寅大統領の虚栄心の強さを示しています。彼は自分の野心のために、韓国を北朝鮮が望むように変えていくでしょう。しかし国の指導者というものは、自分を律しなければなりません。彼は統一のプロセスの端緒に手をつけることだけを考えるべきです。その過程は30年から50年はかかるものであり、文在寅大統領が生きているうちに達成できるようなものではないでしょう。

He is dismantling fortifications along the DMZ. Things like anti-tank obstacles, and guard posts are being removed. He is considering redeploying the 2nd Marine division from the Han river estuary, and the 7th Mechanized Corps from north of Seoul.

彼は実際、非武装地帯の要塞を解体しています。例えば対戦車用障害物や監視所などが撤去されているのです。さらに、漢江河口の第2海兵師団、ソウル北部の第7機械化兵団を移動させようと考えています。

These moves would leave Seoul wide open to a sudden Northern military strike. He is also dismantling the Defense Security Command, and the National Intelligence Service.

これによってソウルは、北朝鮮の奇襲攻撃に対して無防備になります。文大統領は、国軍機務司令部と大韓民国国家情報院も解体しています。

These two organizations track North Korean spies in South Korea.

この二つの組織は、韓国内の北朝鮮工作員を追跡するものです。

第10章　日本と統一コリアの戦争シミュレーションについての解説

North Korea is making no reciprocal moves at all. It is as if President Moon wishes to surrender to North Korea.

北朝鮮は、それに対応するような軍事的脅威の縮小化を、全く行っていません。文在寅大統領は、まるで北朝鮮に降伏することを望んでいるかのようです。

The two Koreas are so different, a long process is the only way unification can work with out war. America and Canada used to be one as British colonies, but they have much more successful chances of unification than the two Koreas. The Americans wouldn't mind, but the Canadians wouldn't like it.

南北二つのコリアはあまりにも差がありすぎるので、戦争せずに統一しようとするならば、長い時間をかけるしかありません。米国とカナダは、かつて一つの英国植民地でしたが、米国とカナダの方が韓国と北朝鮮よりも、はるかに円滑に統一できるでしょう。まあ、米国人が賛成しても、カナダ人は絶対に反対するでしょうけれど。

Also, there are proposals to open navigation on the Han river estuary to civilians. Here is an area where the front line still exists. But opening it to civilian shipping will make it a smugglers paradise between the two Koreas.

それと、漢江河口での民間船舶の航行を許可しようという提案も行われています。ここは非武装地帯の最前線です。ここで民間船舶の航行を許可すれば、密輸業者にとっては楽園となります。

Southern goods will go North, Northern agents will go South. These will increase instability and the chance for loss of control by both Korean governments, and possible rash, panicked decisions.

南の物資が北に入り、北の工作員が南に入ります。それによって、さらに不安定な要素が増え、南北両政府は国を統制できなくなる可

Chapter10 An explanation of the simulation of war between Japan and a newly reunified Korea

能性が高くなり、やはり、無謀で軽率な意思決定をする可能性が高まります。

If the two countries do quickly unify in the newly formed joint military, only Northerners would be trusted with modern aircraft like the F-16. Officers of the Army would be Northerners or politically reliable Southerners, the mixing of Southern units with Northern units would be done to prevent revolt and facilitate control.

この二つの国が統一された場合、新しく創設された軍では、例えばF-16のような新しい航空機は、北のパイロットだけが扱うことになるでしょう。そして、指揮官を旧北朝鮮軍の士官か、思想的に信頼できる旧韓国軍の軍人に限定した上で、南北の部隊が統合されます。これは、兵士の反乱を防ぎ、支配を容易にするためです。

At present North Korean pilots are very inexperienced with actual flying. So I think that more pilots might be retained from the former Southern forces. But they would not be allowed in modern aircraft, probably mostly in a teaching role.

ただ、今の北朝鮮空軍のパイロットは、短い時間しか飛行訓練を受けていません。そのため、旧韓国空軍のパイロットが、そのまま配属される可能性はあります。しかし、新鋭機への搭乗は許可されず、主に飛行教官としての任務が割り当てられるでしょう。

The same for Navy ships -- control would be in the hand of the Northerners. Of course, this would drastically reduce both morale and military efficiency. I think the technology of the former South Korean ships would be very hard for Northerners to understand and master in a short time.

海軍の軍艦も同じで、指揮権は旧北朝鮮の軍人に移るでしょう。当然ながら、士気も、能力も、大幅に低下します。北の士官たちが、

第 10 章　日本と統一コリアの戦争シミュレーションについての解説

短期間のうちに旧韓国海軍の軍艦のテクノロジーを理解し、習得することは、まず無理でしょう。

Who are Korean residents of Japan?
在日コリアンという存在

Of the Koreans resident in Japan, at present about 25% are pro-North. It is surmised that some of them are designated as commandos to act on behalf of North Korea in case of war.

在日コリアンのうち、約25％が朝鮮総連系と言われています。その中には、戦争が起きた場合、北朝鮮側の工作員として行動するよう指示されている者がいると推測されます。

However, I think most of these people would keep a low profile in case of a Japanese/Korean war. The fact is, they are really culturally Japanese.

しかし、その大部分は、目立つような行動は避けると思います。実際のところ、彼らは文化的には日本人と変わりません。

Of those who keep Korean nationality, the pro-North people are educated in Korean, and do speak it. The North does maintain a system of schools throughout Japan. But very few of them have actually been to North Korea.

コリア国籍を持つ人のうち、朝鮮総連系の人たちは朝鮮語で教育され、会話ができます。北朝鮮は日本全国で学校を運営しています。しかし、実際に北朝鮮を訪問する人は、あまりいません。

Those who have returned to North Korea to settle have been treated badly. Basically all their possessions they bring from Japan are confiscated on arrival. There was a movement many years ago to resettle in the North,

Chapter10 An explanation of the simulation of war between Japan and a newly reunified Korea

but it basically died out in the 1960s as the true nature of life in the North became known.

　北朝鮮に帰国した人たちは、ひどい扱いを受けます。基本的に、北朝鮮に到着した時、日本から持ってきた所持品は没収されます。過去に、北朝鮮への帰還事業というものがありましたが、北朝鮮の生活実態が知れわたるようになり、1960年代のうちに、ほぼなくなりました。

The majority of Korean residents in Japan are associated with the South. But most of them do not speak any Korean. A few of my Korean friends who have travelled to South Korea say that the Koreans there treat them with disrespect.

　日本の在日コリアンの大多数は民団系です。しかし彼らはほとんど韓国語ができません。私には在日韓国人の友だちが何人かいますが、彼らは韓国に旅行した時、韓国人から無礼な扱いを受けたと話していました。

Japanese Korean residents processing to return to North Korea.

祖国への帰還手続きを行う在日朝鮮人

Many Korean-Japanese residents do take Japanese nationality. There is family pressure to maintain a Korean identity, but over time more and more Koreans opt to legally become Japanese.

数多くの在日コリアンが日本に帰化しています。コリアのアイデンティティを維持しなければならないという家族の圧力はありますが、法的に日本人になることを選ぶ在日コリアンが増えています。

However to create an incident like I describe in my scenario, for example, blowing up a bridge, it would only take a few individuals to perform such an act of terrorism. It could even be done by Korean agents dispatched for the purpose.

しかし、私が前章のシナリオで書いたような、橋を爆破するなどのテロ行為の実行は、少数の人員で十分可能です。北朝鮮から送り込まれた特殊部隊でも行えます。

The nature of the fighting in Fukuoka city
福岡市付近での戦闘

Once the invasion starts, there could be enough agents infiltrated into Japan plus some Korean residents to create initial havoc in areas around Fukuoka city, blowing up transport links.

日本への侵略が始まった時点で、交通の要所を破壊して福岡市周辺を大混乱に陥れるために、十分な数の北朝鮮特殊部隊、および在日コリアン工作員がその付近にいます。

The distance from the coast of Korea to Japan is short. An invasion fleet could cross in about a day. This would give little warning time. Present day South Korea has a good collection of landing ships, and the North has some.

Chapter10   An explanation of the simulation of war between Japan and a newly reunified Korea

韓国の海岸から日本までは近いので、侵略艦隊は１日で到達できます。警告を発する時間はほとんどありません。韓国は複数の優れた揚陸艦を保有しており、北朝鮮にも数隻あります。

In the Fukuoka city area itself there are no infantry units of the Japanese army. They are some distance away. In the scenario I do not have the Federated Korean Air Force trying to bomb Japanese bases or to provide close air support.

福岡市内には、陸上自衛隊の歩兵部隊はありません。少し離れたところに配備されています。このシナリオでは、コリア連邦軍は自衛隊の基地空爆や近接航空支援を行っていません。

Close air support is an art. You do not want to bomb your own troops. To learn how to drop bombs just a few meters from your own troops takes training and time. In the unified Federated Korean there would be no time for such training. Instead, I think they would concentrate on trying to maintain air superiority of the Tsushima straits.

近接航空支援には高度な技術が必要です。味方を爆撃するわけにはいきません。自軍の兵士から数メートルの距離にある目標にピンポイントで爆弾を命中させるには、長時間の訓練が必要です。コリア連邦軍にはその時間はないでしょう。その代わりにコリア連邦空軍は、対馬海峡の制空権を確保することに力を注ぐだろうと思います。

That is also why the mining operation fails. It is complex, and since virtually all vessels of the Federated Korean Navy would be former Southern ships with mixed crews, their performance would be poor.

同様に、機雷の敷設も失敗します。その作業は複雑だからです。コリア連邦海軍の軍艦は南北混成の乗員なので、そうした能力は劣っているでしょう。

Also, the lack of supply is realistic. It is a historic fact that in most wars with modern weapons ammunition expenditure is underestimated. In a Federated Korean invasion force of 25,000, I think they would find that ammunition supply would soon reach crisis levels, and it would have a direct effect on morale and combat capability.

それと、補給の欠乏は現実的な問題です。近代兵器を用いた戦争のほとんどで弾薬の消費量が過小評価されるのは、歴史的な事実です。コリア連邦軍2万5千の部隊に対する補給はすぐに危機的な状態になり、その士気と戦闘能力に直接影響するでしょう。

In particular, former Southern troops would become disillusioned. With the initial unification of North and South Korea, there would be great euphoria. However, the increasing restrictions of a country which would be adopting a Northern type of restrictive society would tarnish the dream.

特に、南部の兵士の士気は低下してくるでしょう。初めのうちは、民族統一の偉業に強い高揚感が得られます。しかし、統一コリアが北朝鮮のような閉塞的な社会に変貌していくにつれ、当初の希望は失望に変質していきます。

Then, faced with the reality of difficult combat against Japan, I think many of them would choose surrender rather than fight to the death.

自衛隊との激しい戦闘に直面すれば、南部の兵士たちの多くは、死ぬまで戦うよりも降伏を選ぶでしょう。

The effects of Nodong missile attacks
ノドンミサイルによる攻撃

Because bombing inside Japan would be too complex for the newly integrated Air Force, I have them use Nodong missiles to interdict Japanese Army bases in Kyushu. As I have written, most of the former

Chapter10 An explanation of the simulation of war between Japan and a newly reunified Korea

Southern Air Force planes would now be flown by politically reliable Northerners. But they would not have had much time to become familiar with their new aircraft.

統合されたコリア空軍にとって、日本本土への空爆はあまりにも困難な任務となるため、九州の自衛隊基地に対しては、ノドンミサイルが使用されます。すでに述べたように、ほとんどの旧韓国空軍の航空機は、思想的に信頼できる北のパイロットが搭乗します。しかし彼らは、新鋭機に慣熟する時間がありません。

So regarding the missile strikes. In my scenario, they are not very effective. In the 1991 Gulf War, Iraq launched 88 Scud missiles at Israel. 74 Israeli's died, 2 were killed directly, the rest by heart attacks and suffocation. The Nodong is very similar to the Scud.

そのため、ミサイルでの攻撃が行われます。しかし私のシナリオでは、その効果はほとんどありません。1991年の湾岸戦争では、イラクがイスラエルに88発のスカッドミサイルを発射しました。74人が死亡しましたが、ミサイルの直撃で死亡したのは2人、残りは心臓麻痺と窒息死でした。ノドンは、このスカッドミサイルと似ています。

These missiles are highly inaccurate, most would fall in mountain areas. Some would fall into civilian areas outside the bases. So it is my guess that some hundreds would be killed.

このミサイルの命中精度は非常に低く、ほとんどが山地に着弾するでしょう。何発かは基地周辺の一般市民のエリアに着弾しますが、私の推定では、死者は数百人程度です。

Even with the expensive and extensive missile defense system Japan has, most missiles fired in a barrage would get through.

日本は、広範囲をカバーする高価なミサイルシステムを持ってい

ますが、敵から同時に多数のミサイルを発射されると、どうしても撃ち漏らすものが出てきます。

There has been much speculation and fear over these weapons in Japan. They are not that scary. By this I mean, yes, they can kill some people and destroy some buildings, but they cannot destroy Japan.

日本では、このノドンミサイルについて、いろいろな憶測や不安がありますが、実際はそれほど恐ろしい兵器ではありません。まあ、少し犠牲者が出て、いくつか建物が破壊されるでしょうが、日本を崩壊させるようなものではありません。

There is a theory I have about Nodong missiles in North Korea. There are some 600 Hwasong 5-7 missiles, and 450 Nodong missiles in North Korea. Of course this is an estimate. But I do not think that all will fly. Maintenance problems will remove some from the flyable list.

私はこの北朝鮮のノドンミサイルについて、ある推測をしています。北朝鮮には600発のファソン5〜7ミサイル、そして450発のノドンミサイルがあります。もちろん、これは推定です。しかし、全部が発射可能ではないはずです。整備上の問題で発射できないものがあるでしょう。

But I think lack of fuel will be critical. North Korea is an extremely poor country. Fuel is scarce. Most missile facilities are in remote areas. I am guessing local commanders would be tempted to sell fuel on the black market. They would be betting that war would not occur.

私は、燃料不足が重要な問題だと考えています。北朝鮮はとても貧しい国です。燃料が不足しています。ミサイル基地はだいたい、へんぴな地域にあります。そこにいる指揮官は、闇市場で燃料を横流ししようとするんじゃないかと私は想像しています。彼らはおそらく、戦争なんか起こらないと思っています。

Chapter10　An explanation of the simulation of war between Japan and a newly reunified Korea

People might be surprised at my theory, but often, dictatorships have this tendency. As long as local commanders do not make any kind of political moves against the central government, there could be a tendency to ignore criminal activity.

読者は私のこの推測に驚くかもしれませんが、独裁政権では、しばしばこのようなことが起こります。僻地の部隊長が反政府的な行動を取らないかぎり、中央政府は、多少の不正行為であれば黙認するという傾向があるのです。

Command in remote areas of North Korea is where people out of favor are sent. Command in Pyongyang and near Pyongyang are for the most trusted officers.

北朝鮮では、僻地には信頼度の低い者が派遣されます。反対に、平壌やその周辺には、最も信用できる士官が置かれます。

I remember the story of person traveling from Wonsan to Pyongyang. They waited in the train at Wonsan station for three days, the train did not move. Passengers sat waiting in the train cars, because they had no idea when it would actually go. Apparently train schedules are fiction in North Korea.

私は、元山から平壌まで旅行した人の話を思い出します。その乗客は、元山駅の列車の中で３日間、列車が動くのを待っていました。いつ発車するのか全く分からないので、乗客は列車の中で座って待つしかありません。北朝鮮では、列車の時刻表はフィクションなのです。

This person heard of a truck convoy heading for Pyongyang, and decided to ride on that. In the central mountains, they were stopped by Army troops, and robbed of anything of value.

そこで彼は、トラックの一団が平壌に行くと聞いたので、それに

乗せてもらうことにしました。その結果、中央部の山脈で陸軍兵士に止められて、彼が持っていた価値のありそうな物は、全て奪われてしまいました。

In North Korea, in areas away from the capitol, a kind of anarchy reigns. As long as it does not get political, the regime ignores it.

北朝鮮の首都から離れた地域は、ある種の無秩序な状態にあります。しかし反政府的な問題を起こさない限り、政権はそれをとがめません。

Furthermore, a unified Korea is supposedly launching this war to help Korean residents in Japan. Bombarding all of Japan with a missile barrage would be bad for their international image. Also, not all of their missiles would be workable. They would need to keep many in reserve for future contingencies.

私のシナリオでは、統一コリア連邦は、在日コリアンを守るという名目で戦争を開始するという設定になっていますが、さすがに日本全土をミサイルで攻撃するようなことをすると、国際世論にマイナスの影響が出るでしょう。また、全てのミサイルが発射可能なわけでもなく、将来の不測の事態に備えて、予備のミサイルを確保しておく必要もあります。

Would the North Koreans use nuclear weapons?
北朝鮮は核兵器を使用するのか？

I do not think at all that present day North Korea has a workable nuclear weapon. At best, they might have something that could be put in a merchant ship, and have that ship dock in a Japanese harbor and set it off. In case of war, such a method would be entirely impractical.

Chapter10 An explanation of the simulation of war between Japan and a newly reunified Korea

私は、北朝鮮が実用的な核兵器を持っているとは全く考えていません。貨物船に載せて、日本の港に入港させて爆発させるようなことはできるでしょうが、実際の戦争では、これは全く現実性がありません。

In this scenario, I have an American Feminist President not helping Japan because she declares Japan to be patriarchal country. That is one thing. However if Federated Korea used a nuclear weapon on Japan, it would be impossible for America to ignore. America would be forced to respond, or to totally lose trust with other alliance partners.

このシナリオでは、米国のフェミニスト大統領が、日本は女性差別が甚だしいという理由で、日米同盟を守らないと宣言しています。これは一つの可能性です。しかし、コリア連邦が日本に核兵器を使用した場合は、さすがに米国がそれを無視することはないでしょう。米国がそれに対応しなければ、他の同盟国の信用を完全に失うことになるからです。

And Russia, even China, would certainly not be happy with a Federated Korean first use of nuclear weapons. The point is, nuclear weapons are difficult to use as offensive weapons. Federated Korea in this war, wants to conquer at least a portion of Japan for it's own use. They don't want to destroy Japan with nuclear weapons, they would prefer an enslaved Japan.

ロシアも、それに中国でさえ、コリア連邦の核兵器の先制使用を許さないでしょう。要するに、核兵器を先に使用するのは難しいということです。この戦争では、コリア連邦は少なくとも日本の領土の一部を支配することを意図しています。日本を核兵器で壊滅させるのではなく、日本を隷属させることを望んでいるのです。

So even if the present North Korea has workable nuclear weapons, I do not see their use in offensive war. The risk of nuclear response is too great.

ですから、現在北朝鮮が使用可能な核兵器を持っていたとしても、日本への攻撃には使わないと思います。核兵器を使用した場合のリスクが大きすぎます。

The Federated Korean tactic of using obsolete aircraft as a screen for the more modern planes is realistic. It is of course a suicide mission. It is of course difficult to get hard information about North Korean military tactics at this time. But I have read of a plan in wartime to use obsolete aircraft, like the Mig-17, Mig-19, and Mig-21 on suicide missions.

旧式の軍用機を前方展開させるというコリア連邦の戦術は現実的です。もちろんこれは、生きて帰れる可能性がほとんどない任務です。現時点では、北朝鮮の軍事作戦に関する確実な情報を入手することは困難です。しかし、北朝鮮が時代遅れの軍用機、例えば、ミグ17、ミグ19、ミグ21を生還の望みのない任務で使用する計画があるというのは、ニュース記事で読んだことがあります。

They would be fitted out with chemical weapons, and the mission is to fly to Seoul, crash somewhere in the city, and cause chaos.

おそらく北朝鮮のミサイルの弾頭には、化学兵器が搭載されるでしょう。それをソウル市内に着弾させれば、混乱を引き起こすことができます。

The fighting ability of the Self Defense forces and lessons of the First World war
自衛隊の実戦能力と第一次大戦の教訓

Now a few words about the performance of the Japanese Army. First of all, in Japan, the proper term is not Army. We use the word Self Defense Force. Ground Self Defense Force, Air Self Defense Force, and Maritime

Chapter10　An explanation of the simulation of war between Japan and a newly reunified Korea

Self Defense Force.

　ここで、日本の自衛隊の能力について少しお話ししましょう。まず、日本では、公式には「軍隊」という用語を使いません。「自衛隊」という用語を使っています。陸上自衛隊、航空自衛隊、海上自衛隊です。

This is due to the constitution imposed upon Japan by America at the end of WWII. It forbade Japan to have a military. In WWII, many Americans were shocked that a non-white non-Christian country could fight so well.

　これは、大東亜戦争後に、米国から押しつけられた憲法が原因です。この憲法は日本が軍隊を持つことを禁止しています。大東亜戦争では、多くの米国人が、非キリスト教徒の有色人種にすぎない日本人に大いに苦しめられたことにショックを受けました。

It can be said that the post war constitution was pure racism. However, when North Korea invaded South Korea in 1950, it became obvious that for America to maintain it's power in Asia, a full-fledged Japanese military, allied with America was needed. Following that we have the word games going around of what the infamous Article Number 9 in the Constitution says.

　この戦後の憲法は、完全な人種差別の産物でした。しかし、1950年に北朝鮮が韓国に侵攻すると、米国は、アジアでその力を維持するには、米国の同盟下に置いた日本軍の必要性を痛感しました。それで、悪名高い憲法第9条を、解釈で改憲するという言葉遊びが始まりました。

It says that Japan will not maintain armed forces. So they are called Self Defense forces. The Left, and may other people in Japan treat this document as religion. When America created the constitution, they did not understand the power of the written word in Japan.

　憲法には、日本は軍隊を保持しないと書いています。このため彼らは、自衛隊と呼ばれています。日本の左派、あるいはその他の人々も、この憲法を宗教のように信奉しています。米国が憲法を作った時、日本語で書かれたその言葉の威力を理解していませんでした。

Americans change their constitution all the time to fit changing times. There are 33 constitutional amendments. We do not change it. And the Americans intentionally made it difficult to change.

　米国人は時代の変化に合わせて常に憲法を変えます。米国はこれまで 33 回、憲法を改正してきました。日本では憲法を改正するのは困難です。米国人が意図的に改正を困難にしたからです。

America made a great mistake in imposing this constitution on Japan. Well, in the occupation, they insisted on using idealistic people who could not speak Japanese, and knew nothing about Japan. So such a great error is not surprising.

　米国が日本にこの憲法を押しつけたのは大きな間違いでした。まあ、占領下で彼らは、日本語も日本のことも知らない理想主義者を使いましたから。だから、こんな大きな間違いが起きたのです。

Of course, reality is, no modern state can exist without a military to protect it's existence. The problem is many Japanese people just do not understand this reality. The fact is that other countries envy us, and would attack Japan if they could is not understood by Japanese. Time and time again I have had this discussion with very nice people. They just cannot imagine that another country would do something bad to Japan.

　もちろん、現実には、国防を担う軍隊がなければ国家は存続できません。問題は、多くの日本人がこの現実を理解していないということです。日本をねたんでいる国が存在し、状況が許せば彼らはい

Chapter10　An explanation of the simulation of war between Japan and a newly reunified Korea

つでも日本に攻め込んでくる、という現実を理解していません。私はこのことを何度も議論したことがあります。議論の相手は、とても心の優しい人たちです。この人たちは、他の国が日本を侵略するという状況が想像できないのです。

That is not truth, and that is part of the reason I wrote this scenario. It is to show that another country can trap itself into starting war, in this case a unified Korea. If you want a classic example of this, please study how WWI began. Great Britain, France, Germany, and Russia really did not want a major war.

彼らは現実を見ていません。それは私がこのシナリオを書いた理由の一つでもあります。ある国が、戦争をせざるをえない状況に陥るということは、十分にあり得るのです。このシナリオでは、それは統一コリアでした。もし、本当に起こった過去の事例を知りたい場合は、第一次世界大戦がなぜ始まったのかを調べてみてください。実際、英仏独露は大戦争など望んでいませんでした。

They were trapped by alliances and railway timetables. Why the railway timetables? Mobilization of the armies had been pre-planned and set to the exact minute each unit would board it's train to go to the front. Even a one-day halt in this mobilization by a country's army could result in an enemy country with an army ready to fight reaching a border first (provided they are not delayed) and the delayed country would suffer defeat and invasion all because of a timetable error.

これらの国々は、同盟国と、鉄道の時刻表に行動を縛られてしまいました。なぜ鉄道時刻表なのでしょう？　陸軍の動員は以前から計画されており、各部隊が列車に乗って前線に向かう正確な時刻が決まっていました。この時刻表を守らないと、あらゆる方面で動員の計画は頓挫し、一方、時刻表を守った他国は戦闘態勢が整った状態で先に国境に到達します。その結果、自国は敗北と侵略に苦しむことになるのです。

第 10 章　日本と統一コリアの戦争シミュレーションについての解説

So there really was no chance of negotiation. The leaders of these countries, even though they did not want war, were trapped by railway technology. And the war was just about the bloodiest the world has ever seen. Trench warfare was a nightmare.

実際、交渉の機会は本当にありませんでした。これらの国々の指導者たちは、戦争など望んでいなかったのに、鉄道技術に縛られてしまいました。そしてそれは、過去最悪の、最も血にまみれた戦争になりました。特に、塹壕戦は悪夢でした。

Another historical note about WWI. It started as a war of maneuver, but when the German Army failed to take Paris in 1914, it settled into trench warfare. Four long years of trench warfare that became a nightmare of slaughter.

これは、第一次世界大戦についての、もう一つの歴史の豆知識です。この戦争は機動戦で始まりましたが、ドイツ軍は 1914 年にパリを占領できず、膠着して塹壕戦になりました。それは 4 年も続きました。大量の死者を出した悪夢の塹壕戦でした。

But the Western countries had fore-knowledge of the effects of the defense at the time, which they ignored. Great Britain, France, Austria-Hungary, Germany and the United States all sent military observers to the Russo-Japanese war.

しかし当時、西洋諸国は防御陣地をめぐる戦いがどういう結果をもたらすのか、前もって分かっていました。それでも彼らは無視しました。英国、フランス、オーストリア、ハンガリー、ドイツ、米国は、日露戦争に軍のオブザーバーを派遣しています。

They were present at the battle of Port Arthur. At Port Arthur, the Russian port was protected by extensive fortifications, and supported by machine guns and artillery. This caused many casualties upon the attacking Japanese Imperial Army.

彼らはポート・アーサー（旅順）の戦いに立ち会っていたのです。ポート・アーサーでは、ロシアの軍港は広範囲に配置された要塞に守られ、要塞には大量の機関銃と大砲が設置されていました。日本陸軍はそれに対して突撃を敢行し、多数の死傷者を出しました。

Yet the Western observers, in their hubris, discounted this strength of defense fortifications and weaponry. To them, the Russians, even though White and Christian, were looked down upon as inferior. Of, course, through the lens of their racially prejudiced thinking, they thought even less of the Japanese troops.

そういう現実を目の当たりにしたのに、西洋各国の軍のオブザーバーたちは日露両国を見下していたために、要塞とその兵器の防御力の強さを軽視しました。ロシア人は白人でキリスト教徒でしたが、他の西洋列強は、自分たちより劣った連中とみなしていました。有色人種の日本兵などは、当然ながら、さらに見下されていました。

This racial hubris was to cost millions of lives of European soldiers a few years later in WWI.

このような傲慢な意識があったせいで、数年後に勃発した第一次世界大戦で、何百万人ものヨーロッパの兵士が犠牲になったのです。

Today, being in the Japanese military is not very well respected in Japan. Working for a major corporation or the bureaucracy is much more desired. This is in contrast to before WWII, when the military was a highly respected profession.

今の日本では、自衛官になってもあまり尊敬されません。優秀な人材は大企業や官庁に就職しようとします。大東亜戦争以前とは、まるで違います。当時、軍人は非常に尊敬される職業でした。

第 10 章　日本と統一コリアの戦争シミュレーションについての解説

This is because Leftist elements in post WWII Japan have embraced and expanded American wartime propaganda that a Japanese military is inherently evil.

なぜそうなったのかというと、大東亜戦争後、日本の左翼勢力が、日本軍は本質的に邪悪な存在であるという米国の戦時プロパガンダを受け入れ、それを拡散したからです。

I have many Japanese military friends, both active duty and retired. I am a former United States Marine myself, and I look at them with my Marine Corps eyes. They are very competent. And dedicated. Their Japanese-made equipment is top class. In a war, I have no doubt that they will prevail.

私には自衛隊の友だちが、現役にも OB にもたくさんいます。私は元米海兵隊なので、彼らを海兵隊の目で見ます。彼らは非常に有能であり、かつ勇敢です。彼らが扱う日本製の兵器はトップクラスの性能です。戦争において彼らが敵を上回る能力を発揮することを、私は疑いません。

The newest tank of the Ground Self Defense Force, the type 10 medium tank.

陸上自衛隊の最新鋭10式中戦車

Chapter10 An explanation of the simulation of war between Japan and a newly reunified Korea

The possibility of American military revolt
米軍兵士による反乱の可能性

In fact, since the present day US military has been devastated by social justice policies and expensive equipment that doesn't work, I would rate Japan's forces as superior to American.

実際のところ、今の米軍は、社会的公正の導入や、高価なのに欠陥のある兵器のせいで、軍隊としての能力がかなり劣化しています。それで私は、日本の自衛隊は米軍よりも優秀だと評価するのです。

The idea of human shields is not an exaggeration. In 1990, Saddam Hussein used some 800 Europeans, Japanese, and Kuwaiti as human shields by placing them in strategic installations in Iraq.

前章シミュレーションでの、コリア連邦が人間の盾を使う、という話は誇張ではありません。1990年、サダム・フセインが800人のヨーロッパ人、日本人、クウェート人を、工場や製油所などの戦略的重要拠点に配置して、人間の盾として使いました。

I think in urban areas the Japanese Ground Forces would indeed elect to take more casualties themselves than use artillery and airstrikes to destroy the enemy before an infantry assault.

本来の戦闘では、事前の砲爆撃で敵兵力を減殺した後で、歩兵が突入しますが、人間の盾がある場合、自衛隊は、たとえ自衛隊員の犠牲が増えることが分かっていても、事前の砲爆撃は選択しないでしょう。

As for the US Marine revolt in Okinawa, the Marines made the most resistance to the politically correct craziness of the Obama administration. They resisted to the end the concept that women are able to serve in combat roles.

　次に、沖縄で米海兵隊が反乱するというシナリオについてです。海兵隊は、オバマ政権の愚かなポリティカル・コレクト政策に、最も抵抗しました。彼らは、女性も男性と同じように戦闘任務を行えるという意見に、最後まで抵抗しました。

They are not. 25% of the men who took infantry training would fail, as it is an intense course. I myself was not assigned to the infantry, so I only had two weeks of infantry training in basic training. It was arduous.

　実際、女性に戦闘任務は無理です。海兵隊で歩兵コースを選んだ男性の25％が合格できないのです。私は歩兵コースを選択しなかったので、2週間の基礎訓練しか受けていませんが、それでも恐ろしいほど厳しい訓練でした。

I think the idea of Marines revolting against such politically correct leadership is realistic.

　そのような海兵隊が、ポリティカル・コレクトな指導者に反抗したのは、当然のことだと思います。

However, when I write of 3rd Marine division units revolting against the US government and coming to the rescue of Japan in a war against Federated Korea, Japanese people should please think again.

　次に、第3海兵師団が米国政府に対して反乱を起こし、日本を助けにくるという設定についてですが、そのことについて、日本人はよく考えてみる必要があります。

In Okinawa there are only the 4th Marine infantry regiment, and the 12th Marine artillery regiment. And in such a simulation as this war, they would have no replacements. That would mean only about 4,000 fighting men.

Chapter10 An explanation of the simulation of war between Japan and a newly reunified Korea

沖縄には、海兵隊の第4海兵連隊（歩兵）、第12海兵連隊（砲兵）しかありません。このシミュレーションでは、彼らには交代要員がいないため、戦闘に参加できる兵員は4千人ほどしかありません。

A word about American troops. If they had been in the battle of Fukuoka, the city would have been destroyed, and many Japanese people killed. Americans use massive artillery barrages and airstrikes. The most important thing for them is the preservation of the lives of their own troops.

そして、もし米軍が福岡の戦いに参加したら、街は破壊され、多くの一般市民が死ぬことになるでしょう。米軍は事前の砲爆撃を徹底的に行います。彼らにとって最も大切なのは、自軍の兵士の命です。

The preservation of Japanese civilian lives would be secondary.

日本国民の命は二の次です。

That was very evident in the WWII battle of Manila, where American troops took one month to take the city, pulverized it, and 100,000 Philippine civilians died.

それは、大東亜戦争におけるマニラの戦いを見ればはっきり分かります。米国はマニラを占領するにあたって、まず1カ月かけて街を徹底的に破壊しました。このため、10万人ものフィリピン人が死にました。

And a Russian Airborne division is about 5,000 to 7,000 men.

一方、ロシアの空挺師団は5千〜7千人の規模です。

These forces would only have a symbolic value in fighting the Korean invaders or an invasion of Korea.

ただ、この部隊については、ロシアもコリア連邦との戦いに参戦

した、という象徴的な価値しかないでしょう。

The Korean exile army would have quickly formed, and no matter how many in numbers, it would not have had time to coalesce into a truly combat capable army. And it would be numerically small.

亡命韓国軍はすぐに結成されるでしょうが、戦闘可能な部隊に合流する時間がありません。それに、兵士の数も全然足らないでしょう。

So the bulk of the fighting would done by the Japanese Self Defense Forces. And they are quite capable of doing so.

このため、戦闘の大部分は自衛隊が行うことになります。しかし、自衛隊には十分その能力があります。

The people of unified Korea would suffer the most
最も苦しむのは統一コリアの国民たち

The big loser would be the Korean people. This scenario is not hate speech. I am not at all saying that Korean people are inferior in any way. What I am writing is, that a quick unification based on emotion would be a disaster.

結局のところ、最も苦しむ国民は、コリアンです。繰り返しますが、このシナリオはヘイトスピーチではありません。私は、コリアの国民が劣っている、などと言っているわけではありません。私が主張しているのは、統一ムードに酔いしれて性急な統一をすると大きな災厄に見舞われる、ということです。

And that leaders in panic would choose to assault Japan, in a war they could not win. This is just like the leaders of major European nations in 1914, the example I mentioned earlier. They understood they were

Chapter10　An explanation of the simulation of war between Japan and a newly reunified Korea

hurtling towards a war they did not want. Yet because of the technology of mobilization using railroads, they could not stop it for fear of destroying their own countries.

そして、どうしようもなくなった指導者たちというのは、たとえ勝てる見込みがなくとも、日本を攻撃することを選ぶ、ということです。私が紹介した、1914年のヨーロッパの大国の指導者たちの場合と同じです。彼らも、誰も望まぬ戦争に向かって進んでいることは分かっていました。しかし、簡単には止められない鉄道の技術を使って動員する仕組みだったので、彼らは戦争を止めることができなかったのです。

In the rush to unify North and South Korea, great chaos would result -- that is guaranteed. One solution is to go slowly, very slowly. I think one condition should be that people of both nations be able to freely travel to each nation and return.

北朝鮮と韓国が統一を急ぐと、大混乱に陥ることは確実です。一つの解決策は、統一までに長い時間をかけることです。まずは両国の国民がお互いに自由に行き来できるようになる、というのが一つの条件です。

This could take 30 or 50 years. But it is more realistic. North Korea above all things, wants to preserve it's government. This is understandable. Right now without the Kim family, North Korea would quickly descend into warlordism. I don't think China would want that situation either, as it would result in many refugees crossing into China.

それには、30年から50年かかるでしょう。しかし、それが現実的な方法なのです。何よりも北朝鮮は、自分たちの政府を残したいと考えています。私にもこれは理解できます。金ファミリーがなくなれば、北朝鮮はすぐに軍閥主義になります。中国もそのことには反対でしょう。多くの難民が中国に押し寄せてくるからです。

第 10 章　日本と統一コリアの戦争シミュレーションについての解説

It is Leftists in South Korea that are creating the great trap in this situation. Years and years of anti-Japan propaganda has had it's effect. The Comfort Women issue has become something like a religious cult. If a South Korean would question this narrative, it could result in death. South Koreans have been killed for saying that the annexation period with Japan was not so bad.

この、南北統一という状況においては、韓国左派による長年にわたる反日プロパガンダが、重大な影響を及ぼすことになります。今や慰安婦問題は、宗教カルトのようなものになっています。韓国人がその問題に疑問を投げかけると、その人は殺される可能性すらあります。実際、日本に併合された時代はそんなに悪くなかったと言って、殺された韓国人がいます。

And as I write this, in the summer of 2018, President Moon of South Korea is beginning to give in to North Korea. He has recently announced that he will reduce the Army by 118,000 troops to 365,000 ground troops by 2021. He will also reduce the number of generals from 436 to 360 by 2022.

私がこの文章を書いたのは 2018 年の夏ですが、すでに韓国の文在寅大統領は、北朝鮮に屈し始めています。政府は 2021 年までに陸軍の人員を 11 万 8 千人削減し、36 万 5 千人にすると発表しました。将官の数も、436 人から 360 人まで減らすということです。

This is a strong sign of his pro-Northern sympathies. North Korea has made no matching concession to reduce troop numbers, so this can only weaken the South to the advantage of the North. If fact, propaganda in the North is increasing to state how North Korea is the most wonderful country in the world, even if they have to tighten their belts. I think this propaganda is aimed at dealing with increased contact with Southerners.

これは、彼が北朝鮮に傾倒していることを示す強いサインです。

一方の北朝鮮は、それに見合うような兵力削減を全く行っていません。単に韓国の軍事力が弱体化し、相対的に北朝鮮を軍事的に有利にするだけです。実際、北朝鮮では、たとえ生活は苦しくとも北朝鮮が世界で最も素晴らしい国なのだ、というプロパガンダは増えています。このプロパガンダは、今後、韓国人との交流が増えるという事態に対処するために行っているのだと思います。

And we can assume that the generals eliminated will be those that President Moon feels are conservative, and might mount a coup d'etat.

文在寅大統領が多くの将官を排除したのは、彼らは保守主義者であり、クーデターを起こす可能性があると判断したからだと考えられます。

North Korean commandos and the Gwangju incident
北朝鮮工作員による光州事件

In 1980 there was an uprising in Gwangju, in southwestern South Korea. The world believes this was popular uprising, which led to the end of military rule in South Korea.

1980年、韓国南西部の光州市で暴動がありました。世界は、これを民衆の蜂起だとし、それが韓国の軍事政権の終焉につながったと考えています。

That is not true. The people who conducted the uprising were infiltrators from the North. There were some 1,200 of them. They were split into a 600-man combat force, with a 600-person political action movement. 100,000 troops were in reserve in Haeju North Korea in case the operation succeeded.

しかしそれは事実ではありません。そこで蜂起した人々のうち、

第 10 章　日本と統一コリアの戦争シミュレーションについての解説

1,200 人が北朝鮮からの潜入者でした。彼らのうち 600 人が戦闘部隊、残り 600 人が政治活動部隊であり、この作戦が成功した場合に備えて、北朝鮮の海州市には 10 万の兵士が待機していました。

The combat force ambushed the headquarters element of the 20th infantry division while it was on the move. They stole the vehicles, and used them to steal more vehicles from a nearby factory.

まず、戦闘部隊は移動中の第 20 歩兵師団司令部の部隊を待ち伏せしました。彼らは車両を盗み、その車両を使って近くの工場でさらに車両を盗みました。

They then raided armories around the area. However, the combat unit decimated itself in several frontal assaults against a guarded prison. South Koreans troops began to respond, and the rebellion fell apart.

それから彼らは、その地域にある兵器庫を襲いました。しかし、警護された刑務所を正面から攻撃したことで、逆にかなりの損害を出しました。徐々に韓国軍は態勢を整え始め、反乱側は崩壊していきました。

These actions lead me to believe they had much up to date intelligence on South Korean Army movements.

この戦闘で、おそらく北朝鮮の工作員は、韓国軍の部隊移動に関する最新の情報を得たのだと思います。

It is assumed that the surviving North Koreans were evacuated by ship.

生き残った北朝鮮工作員は、船で避難したと考えられています。

This is quite some number of people involved in this operation. They would have had to have been smuggled in small numbers over a long period of time, and hidden in the area.

Chapter10 An explanation of the simulation of war between Japan and a newly reunified Korea

　この作戦に関わった北朝鮮工作員は大勢いました。彼らは長い時間をかけて徐々に人数を増やし、その地域に潜伏していたに違いありません。

The Southwest of Korea has long had Communistic sympathies. During the Korean war of 1950 to 1953, Communist guerrillas there continued to fight until 1956.

　韓国の南西部には、昔から共産主義に共感する者が多くいます。1950年から53年の朝鮮戦争の期間も、その周辺に共産ゲリラが出没していましたが、彼らは1956年まで戦闘を続けました。

This just proves that North Korea has not ever given up efforts to overcome the South. They cannot do it now by overt military assault. But either President Moon Jae In is very naive, or an out-and-out Leftist who desires Communism. After the Gwangju incident, Several far Left Presidents of South Korea have appointed many Leftists in the South Korean government.

　これは、北朝鮮が韓国を征服する努力を放棄していないということを示しています。彼らは現在、あからさまな軍事攻撃でそれを実行することはできません。しかし、韓国の文在寅大統領はだまされやすい人間なのか、それとも共産主義を望む極左なのでしょうか、光州事件の後、文在寅大統領を含む左派系の大統領たちは、多くの左派の官僚を任命して、政府機関内に送り込みました。

And it is from this time that anti-Japanese education began in schools, and increased in virulence. So a war between Japan and a newly unified Korea is indeed probable.

　そして、この時期から学校教育の現場で反日教育が始まり、日本に対する憎悪が高まりました。それが、統一コリアと日本との間の戦争に現実味を持たせるのです。

Yet South Korea, behind the scenes, continues to rely on Japanese economic aid.

でも裏では、韓国は依然として日本の経済的な協力に依存し続けています。

What South Korean government leaders must try to do in the future is to find a way to cease anti-Japan propaganda. They must cease demanding apologies for claimed wrongs that did not happen. Japan is the only natural partner for Korea.

韓国の政府指導者たちが将来しなければならないのは、反日プロパガンダをやめるという道筋を見出すことです。そして、ありもしないことで言いがかりをつけて謝罪を要求するようなことを、やめなければなりません。韓国にとって、適切なパートナーは日本しかいないのです。

North Korea must find a way to open relations with Japan. One of the biggest things they could do would be to finally provide an accounting of the Japanese citizens abducted to North Korea.

北朝鮮も、日本と関係を改善する道筋を見出さなければなりません。彼らができる最も重要なことは、拉致被害者の問題を完全に解決することでしょう。

These actions are very difficult for the North Koreans, a very proud people. This I understand. But the North agreed to a historic meeting with President Trump. To me, that shows that they are in a very seriously bad condition.

これらの行動が、自尊心の高い民族にとって難しいことは分かります。しかし、北朝鮮は米国のトランプ大統領と歴史的な会談を行うことに合意し、実現しました。それは同時に、北朝鮮はかなり追い詰められた状態であることを示すものです。

It will be a very difficult balancing act in the future. The power of America is definitely waning.

将来も、非常に困難な綱渡りのような行動を取らざるを得ない状況が続くでしょう。そして、米国の力は確実に弱まっていきます。

Unified Korea and China
統一コリアと中国

In reality, although, I think China would try to use a Japanese/Korean war to it's advantage. I don't think China is absolutely set on war with Japan.

現実問題として、中国はコリアと日本の戦争を自己の利益のために利用すると思いますが、中国が日本と直接戦火を交えるようなことは絶対にないと思います。

President Trump and Kim Jong Un in conference.

トランプ大統領と金正恩の会談

第 10 章　日本と統一コリアの戦争シミュレーションについての解説

If China could be certain of a unified Korea without American troops on the Chinese border, I think that would be satisfactory for them.

中国は、統一コリアとの国境近辺に米軍が駐留しないという確証が得られるのなら、それで満足するだろうと思います。

Korean unification is going to take a lot of common work between Japan, China, and Russia.

コリアの統一には、日本、ロシア、中国の協力も必要です。

Many well-meaning people think America will militarily protect Japan. However, is American society capable, or stable enough? What about the American military? Americans always boast about it being the best military in the world, but is that still true?

多くの善意の人々が、米国は日本を軍事的に守ってくれると考えています。しかし、米国の社会は、それが可能なほど安定しているでしょうか？　米国の軍隊はどうでしょう？　米国人はいつも、彼らは世界最強の軍隊だと自慢していますが、今もそうでしょうか？

The truth is, the American military has been seriously damaged by social justice policies created by Feminists and enforced by the Obama administration. It is no longer a powerful military, but a weak shell. If America faced a difficult opponent, such as Russia, China, North Korea or Iran, defeat in battle is certain.

実際はこうです。フェミニストたちが作り出し、オバマ政権が実施した社会的公正政策によって、米軍は深刻なダメージを受けています。米軍はもはや強力な軍隊ではなく、見せ掛けだけのものにすぎません。米国がロシア、中国、北朝鮮、あるいはイランなどの面倒な相手と戦った場合、敗北は必至です。

I have just written a simulation of a possible future war. But Japan is already at war. New Comfort Women statues appear in different countries constantly. The people behind this effort claim this campaign is about international women's rights. Yet they never, ever mention the actual abuse of women on battlefields in such places as Bosnia from 1992 to 1995. Or what Korean troops did in Vietnam during that war.

私は本書で、将来起こり得る戦争のシミュレーションを描きました。しかし現実には、日本はすでに戦争状態にあります。新しい慰安婦像がいくつもの国に次々と建てられています。この運動の支持者たちは、このキャンペーンは世界中の女性の権利を守るためのものだと主張しています。しかし、1992年から1995年まで続いたボスニア紛争での、女性に対するレイプや虐待については、彼らは何も語りません。韓国軍がベトナム戦争で何をしたか、という問題にも沈黙しています。

This Comfort Women campaign is directed squarely at Japan, and it is highly exaggerated. The truth is nowhere near the horrors as described as what has happened. However, it is a coordinated campaign with central direction. It is similar to the culture wars of America. In fact, I suspect that the central direction is the same.

この慰安婦キャンペーンは日本だけを対象にしており、また、あまりにも誇張されています。実際には、彼らが主張するようなことは全くありませんでした。これは組織的なキャンペーンであって、それを指示している中心的な存在があるのです。これは、米国の文化戦争と似ています。おそらく、それを仕掛けている中心的な存在は同じだと思います。

In the United States, this has long been going on with such issues as increased rights for sexual minorities being pushed by Leftists. This is beginning to come to Japan. The goal is the complete destruction of present Japanese and American society. This is not a simple casual social movement. It is directed with goals.

第10章　日本と統一コリアの戦争シミュレーションについての解説

　米国では、こうした混乱が長いあいだ続いており、例えば性的マイノリティの権利などの問題を左派が推進しています。そしてこれは、すでに日本にも上陸し始めています。その目的は、米国や日本の社会をめちゃくちゃにすることです。これは自然発生的な、ただの社会運動ではありません。中心的な存在が目標を定め、指示を出しているのです。

Leftist forces are pushing this, and what we see in America now we can expect in Japan in a few years. Japanese culture is exquisite and refined. Yet the Left wishes to destroy it.

　左派勢力がこれを強く推し進めており、現在米国で起きている問題は、数年後には日本でも起きているでしょう。日本の文化は素晴らしく、洗練されています。しかし、左派はそれを壊したいのです。

The objective of the Left is to destroy the center. Thus in America, there are constant attacks on straight males who are White, and of European descent. This is what is pushing America close to Civil War. The Left is trying to create a society of different and mutually hostile sex-based and ethnic-based tribes constantly in conflict with one another.

　左派の目的は、社会の中心にある核を破壊することです。それで、米国では、ヨーロッパ系で異性愛の白人男性が絶えず攻撃されています。その攻撃により、米国では内戦が近づいています。左派は、性や民族の異なる集団どうしの対立を常態化させ、社会を分断しようとしているのです。

In Japan, it can be argued that Japanese culture goes back to the beginning of the Jomon era, some 16,000 years ago. Gradually, it has evolved where today we have a state with the longest running monarchy in the world. The Emperor is the central pillar of Japan.

　日本の文化は1万6千年前の縄文時代にまでさかのぼることが

できます。そこから長い時を経て、日本は現在、世界最古の皇室がある国となりました。天皇陛下は日本の中心にある柱です。

Yet we are under attack. The Japanese Left is embracing both the Trans-Gender Rights issue and the Feminist "#metoo" movement.

その日本が、攻撃を受けているのです。日本の左派は、トランスジェンダー運動と、フェミニストによる「#metoo」(私もセクハラを受けた) 運動を取り入れています。

Who would benefit from war?
誰がこの戦争で得をするのか？

In this book, I will show what is happening in America, and what we can very soon expect in Japan. And some ideas on how to fight this and preserve this country.

本書では、いま米国で何が起きているのか、そして、日本で近いうちに起きる可能性のある戦争について説明しました。また、それに対してどうやって戦い、日本を守るのかについて、シミュレーション内でいくつか示しています。

And what nation could be directing this? I have no proof yet, but sometimes, in a murder, the detective cannot find proof of a suspect. So where to start? Look for who benefits from the murder.

そもそも一体どの国が、こうした活動を指示しているのでしょうか？ 私はまだ、証拠をつかんでいません。殺人事件でも、犯人を示す証拠が見つからないことがあります。その場合、どこから捜査を始めますか？ まず見当をつけるのは、その殺人事件で利益を得る人物です。

第 10 章　日本と統一コリアの戦争シミュレーションについての解説

In this case, we should look for a country that benefits from all this internal disorder and chaos in America, which is also coming to Japan. The chaos in America is being done by Americans, and they cooperate with Koreans in attacking Japan over history and culture on the world stage.

私たちは、いま米国内で起きている、そして近い将来、日本国内で起きる社会の混乱で、どの国が利益を得るのかを、考える必要があります。米国内の混乱は米国人によるものですが、それと同時に彼らは、韓国人と協力し、日本に対して、世界を舞台にした歴史戦、文化戦を仕掛けているのです。

But I think some country is encouraging them. So look for who would benefit.

私はその背後に、ある国が存在すると考えています。利益を得る国を探しましょう。

I think Japan is worth fighting for.

日本は守る価値のある、素晴らしい国です。

Afterward
おわりに

From what I have written in this book, people might think that I revere war. Not at all. Since the military trains people for war, military people, even those who have not experienced war, have some idea what it is about.

本書の内容を見て、私のことを軍国主義者のように思う人がいるかもしれません。しかしそれは違います。軍人というものは、戦争に備えて訓練しているので、実戦経験がなくとも、戦争とはどのようなものかを理解しているのです。

After all, we are trained for it. There are people who are as the phrase goes, "natural born killers". These are people who love violence, and can be considered mentally ill.

まあ、確かに私たちは戦争するために訓練をしています。世の中には、俗に言う「ナチュラル・ボーン・キラー（生まれつきの人殺し）」という人たちがいます。彼らは暴力を愛する人であり、精神的に病んだ人だと見なすことができます。

But military training is designed to weed these people out. People like that are out of control. What the military teaches you is discipline and control. After all, a military man only acts on orders from designated authority. That is from the nation, the state. He does not act on his own emotions.

しかし、軍事訓練というものは、こういう人たちを排除するように考えられています。そのような人たちは制御することができません。軍隊で教え込まれるのは、規律や統制です。結局のところ、軍人と

いうのは、上官の命令でのみ動きます。それは、つきつめれば国家の命令です。自分の感情に基づいて行動するのではありません。

Japan has many people who are sincere in their desire for peace. Yet they do not know about the reality of war.

日本には、心から平和を願っている人たちが大勢います。しかし彼らは、戦争の現実というものを分かっていません。

War is prevented through military strength. In the simulation of a future Federated Korean invasion of Fukuoka, if Japanese Army forces with anti-ship artillery and ground-based anti-ship missile units, along with anti-air units at the airport, and a nearby infantry regiment, the Federated Korean invasion of Fukuoka could not happen.

戦争は軍事力によって抑止されるのです。コリア連邦が福岡に上陸するシミュレーションにおいても、陸上自衛隊が対艦用の砲兵や地対艦ミサイルの部隊を持ち、そして空港には対空火器が配備され、近くに歩兵連隊が存在していたら、敵の上陸は不可能です。

An invasion in a more isolated part of Kyushu would not have the same political impact. And the Federated Korean government would definitely be depending upon Japanese Leftists to give up fighting and force the Japanese government to make peace on Korean terms.

だからといって、九州の僻地に侵攻しても、同じような政治的なインパクトはありません。その場合コリア連邦は、間違いなく日本の左派を利用し、日本は戦いをやめて、コリアに有利な平和条約を結ぶよう、日本政府に圧力をかけるでしょう。

Recently many abandoned North Korean boats are washing up on Japanese shores. Are agents being infiltrated? There are many boats, and few bodies being found. The possibility certainly exists. I think the present North Korean government is very aware that North Koreans living in Japan may not be reliable saboteurs in a crisis.

最近、北朝鮮の船が日本の海岸に多数漂着しています。工作員が日本に侵入しているのでしょうか？ 多数の船が見つかっていますが、死体はほとんど見つかりません。工作員が上陸している可能性は確かにあります。北朝鮮政府は、有事の際、在日コリアンは工作員として信頼性に乏しいと認識していると思います。

However the sad fact is that naive Japanese people who are anti-war, would give encouragement for such an invasion. A desperate enemy, like the fictional Federated Korea in the simulation, might believe that these Japanese would just give up, or even help in case of an invasion. Then they might think the risky nature of such an invasion could be worth the try.

残念なことに、反戦平和を唱える、常識の欠如した日本人は、逆にこうした侵略を助長してしまいます。私のシミュレーションにおける、架空のコリア連邦のような国が内政上の理由で攻めてくる時、敵は、こういう日本人はすぐに降参して手をあげるか、侵略軍の手助けさえすると思っているかもしれません。だからこそ、敵はこの冒険的な侵略を試してみる価値があると考えるかもしれないのです。

People of Japan today have in general a very low opinion of those in the military. When I joined the United States Marine Corps in 1974, there was a phrase common in American English that I like. It was called "joining the service". It meant to join the military. Another word for the military was "The Service".

今の日本人の多くは、自衛隊の重要性をあまり認識していません。1974年、私が海兵隊に入隊した時、米国英語でよく使われた表現がありました。それは、「奉仕する」です。これは、軍隊に入るという意味です。軍隊を意味するもう一つの言葉は「奉仕」でした。

おわりに

It meant that to join the military was to sacrifice comfort of life for the nation. And even perhaps your own life. It was an act of dedication to the well being of the nation. Something not done for selfish purposes. Until the Vietnam war, it was something that all American young men were expected to do, at least for a few years.

軍隊に入るというのは、国のために自分が快適な生活を送ることを犠牲にする、という意味なのです。時には自分の命を犠牲にする可能性もあります。それは、国民のための献身的な行為であり、利己的な目的で行われるものではありません。ベトナム戦争までは、米国の青年は全て、少なくとも数年間、このような奉仕を行うのが当たり前でした。

Well, that word has now disappeared. Starting with the Vietnam war anti-war protests, Leftists agitators have steadily eroded the basic morality of American life. Now we have a nation at war with itself.

ただ、その言葉はもう消えてしまいました。ベトナム反戦運動から始まり、左派の活動家は徐々に、そうした米国の基本的な道徳を侵食していきました。繰り返すように、今の米国は、内戦のような状態です。

If you look closely at what the American Left is doing, it is promoting extreme selfishness, and dividing American society into groups hostile to each other.

米国の左派の活動をよく見ていると、度を超した利己主義を促進し、米国社会を互いに敵対する集団に分裂させようとしているのが分かります。

I do not think that this can be resolved without extreme violence. Yet there is still hope for Japan. If war does come, for example like in my simulation of a desperate, newly unified Korea invading Japan, I think the

Afterward

reaction of Japanese people would be to protect their land, their nation.

この状況は、もう暴力を抜きにして解決できるとは思えません。しかし、日本にはまだ望みがあります。もしも日本が戦争になったら、私が描いた統一コリアによる日本侵略シミュレーションのように、日本人は自分の領土、自分の国を守る、という行動をとるでしょう。

The Japanese Left would quickly become silent out of shock. Many people would volunteer for the Japanese Armed Forces. People of the Japanese Left might be surprised that I write this. However, that is a common reaction throughout history in nations that have been invaded.

日本の左派はこれに衝撃を受けて、すぐに沈黙するでしょう。多くの人が自衛隊に志願し、日本の左派は、そのことに驚くかもしれません。でもそれは、歴史を見れば、侵略された国々に共通する反応であることが分かります。

That is why the American Roosevelt administration provoked Japan to attack Pearl Harbor. Frankly, the US Naval Intelligence tracked the Japanese fleet approaching Pearl Harbor by radio transmissions.

だからこそ、米国のルーズベルト大統領は、日本に第一撃を撃たせるよう仕向けました。米国海軍情報部は、真珠湾に接近している日本の機動部隊を、その無線交信で追跡していました。

Americans at the time were not at all interested in war. Yet the shock of the Pearl Harbor attack caused a great increase in patriotic spirit throughout the nation. So the Roosevelt administration manipulated it to happen that way.

当時の米国人は、戦争に全く興味がありませんでした。しかし、真珠湾の衝撃は、米国民の愛国心を大いに高める結果となりました。ルーズベルト政権は、民心を巧みに操作したのです。

おわりに

The same would happen in Japan, in the case of a Korean attack. The Japanese Left would instantly lose power and influence. Koreans should beware of this.

コリアによる日本への攻撃でも、同じことが起きます。日本の左翼は即座に、立場も影響力も失います。コリアンは、このことに留意するべきです。

And a word to Koreans. Recent actions that you are doing in your country are leading to war between Korea and Japan. You cannot win this war. I have been seeing comments on social media that say things like, "Korea may have to punish Japan militarily over history issues, and since Japan does not understand history, Japan will lose."

ここで、韓国人に一言。最近韓国で彼らが行っていることは、韓国を日本との戦争に導くものです。この戦争で韓国が勝つことは不可能です。私はソーシャルメディアで、次のようなコメントを見てきました。歴史問題で反省しない日本を、韓国は武力で懲らしめなければならない、日本が正しい歴史を理解しないなら、日本は叩きのめされることになる、と。

This is insane babble, but in an increasingly tense situation, such thinking is dangerous.

これは、頭のおかしな人の放言のようなものですが、緊張が高まりつつある状況では、このような考え方は非常に危険なのです。

The abrogation of the 2015 Comfort Women agreement has inspired disgust with Korea internationally. Again, social media comments by people of many nations go overwhelmingly against Korea on this issue.

韓国は2015年の慰安婦合意を破棄しましたが、世界はこうした韓国のやり方に対して、うんざりしています。この問題についてソーシャルメディアで多くの国の人たちのコメントを見ても、圧倒的に

Afterward

韓国に対して批判的です。

Now Koreans are suing Japanese companies over labor issues during WWII. Again, foreigners do not respect this. In a war, many things happen.

現在、韓国人が大東亜戦争中の労働問題で、日本企業を訴えています。外国人はこれについても韓国に同情していません。戦争では、いろいろなことが起きるのです。

For example, the American bombing of Japan was indeed genocidal in nature. But Japanese people today do not continually demand compensation from Americans. Instead, Japanese look for ways to work with America in international cooperation.

例えば、大東亜戦争での米国の日本本土空襲は、事実上の大虐殺でした。しかし、今の日本人は、米国人に補償を要求し続けるようなことはしていません。逆に、日本人は国際協力において米国人と連携しようとしています。

Other countries have difficulties with their neighbors. Nobody is really interested in Korea's problem. You are not the center of the world.

他の国々も、隣国との間では問題を抱えています。他国はどこも、韓国の問題には興味がありません。韓国は世界の中心ではないのです。

And those problems are imaginary. Other people do know the history of WWII, and Korea had a very benign experience. Japan simply did not commit the horrors that you say happened. The truth is Japan did many wonderful things for Korea.

そして、彼らの主張する問題は空想の産物です。韓国人以外の人たちは、第二次世界大戦の歴史を知っています。当時の朝鮮は、厳しい戦争など体験していないということも。今の韓国人が主張する

おわりに

ような恐ろしいことを、日本は行っていません。逆です。実際は、日本は朝鮮のために素晴らしいことをたくさん行ったのです。

Well, America also is being hijacked by crazed social activists, who are pushing such ideas as men can be women by just declaring that they are. That scientific biological differences between men and women do not exist.

まあ、現在は米国も狂った社会活動家に乗っ取られていて、彼らは、自分で宣言するだけで男性が女性になれるような社会を作ろうとしています。彼らは、男女の間に生物学的な違いなど存在しないと言っています。

The majority of Americans are becoming angered by such social activism, thus we have the election of President Trump. And I am seeing evidence that many Koreans are becoming angry at the hysteria of this anti-Japan crusade in Korea.

しかし、大多数の米国人はそうした社会運動に対して怒りを感じているので、トランプ大統領が当選しました。そして私は、韓国人の中に、反日ヒステリーに怒っている人たちが多数いる、ということを知っています。

And you only hurt yourselves. Recently, a collaborative business venture between the Mitsui group and the Korean company Shinsegae, in making health foods, was canceled. The reason was protest by Korean activists, since the Mitsui group is being targeted in WWII labor suits.

ただし、損をするのは韓国人なのです。最近、三井物産と韓国の新世界フードの、健康食品に関する共同事業が中止になりました。戦時中の労働問題で三井は戦犯企業だという理由で、韓国の活動家たちが抗議したからです。

Just think of how many Koreans might have found employment in this joint venture! Yet now it won't happen. Your activists are destroying your own society. These activists are pushing Korea into a fast unification between the North and South which will be a disaster. The anti-Japan hysteria that they are creating may very well lead to a war which will be a disaster.

本来なら、このジョイントベンチャーに、多くの韓国人が就職できたことでしょう。でも、もうダメです。韓国の活動家は、自分の国を崩壊させています。こうした活動家たちが、北と南の統一を性急に進めて、大失敗することは目に見えています。彼らが作り出した反日のヒステリーは、戦争に導くことになるかもしれません。しかしそれは、南北コリアに大惨事を招きます。

It is time for the sane Koreans to regain control of their country.

良識の残っている韓国人が韓国を取り戻すべき時が来ているのです。

Now a few words for American people. It is time to stop thinking of Japan in terms of The Pacific War, and to be more realistic. While more Americans are taking a more positive view of Japan, too many still think negatively about Japan.

次に、米国人に一言。そろそろ、大東亜戦争の時代で日本を考えることはやめるべきです。そして、もっと現実的に考えるべきです。日本のことを前向きにとらえる米国人は増えていますが、それでもまだ、日本を否定的に考える米国人が多過ぎます。

Japan never was the horror that German Nazism was. It is time to forget the wartime propaganda. Japan is probably the most steadfast friend of the United States in Asia, without Japan, America's power stops just west of Hawaii. Never forget that.

日本は、ナチスドイツのような恐ろしい国ではありませんでした。もう、戦争時代のプロパガンダは忘れるべきです。アジアにおいて

おわりに

日本は、米国の最も不動の友好国でしょう。日本がいなければ、米国の権力はハワイよりちょっと西にしか及びません。それを忘れてはダメなのです。

And to the people of Japan. It is time to wake up. In the 45 years I have lived here, I have seen that concerning international affairs, most Japanese are living in dream like world, a fairy tale. They believe that as long as we trust in America, everything will be fine.

そして日本国民よ！ 今こそ目覚める時です。私は日本に 45 年間住んで、こと国際問題に関しては、ほとんどの日本人が夢の世界、おとぎ話の世界に生きているように見えています。彼らは、米国を信用していれば何の問題もないと考えているのです。

Well, now reality intrudes, rudely. America is collapsing from within, and the American ability to influence world events is declining rapidly.

これから、厳しい現実が押し寄せてきます。米国は国内から崩壊し、世界各地で起こる事態に対する影響力は、急速に弱まっていきます。

The family is the basic block of society, and a Nation is like an extended family. It is time for Japanese people themselves to defend this Nation, this extended family. We cannot depend on any other nation to do this.

家族というのは社会の基礎であり、国というのは巨大な家族なのです。今や、日本人自身がこの国、この大きな家族を守るべき時なのです。もう、他国に頼ることはできません。

Japan is one of the more powerful nations in the world, and to my experience, Japanese people are by far the most innovative. It is time for everyone to wake up, and to do their best.

日本は、世界で最も力を持った国であり、私の知る限り日本人は、

Afterward

世界で最も革新的な人たちです。今こそ、皆が目覚め、自分たちのベストを尽くすべき時なのです。

We must protect our extended family, our nation, by ourselves.

私たちは、私たちのこの大きな家族、自分の国を、自分たちの力で守らなくてはなりません。

マックス・フォン・シュラー

Special Thanks to Matt Bigelow, my English proofreader!

◆著者◆
マックス・フォン・シュラー（Max von Schuler）

本名、マックス・フォン・シュラー小林。
元海兵隊・歴史研究家。ドイツ系アメリカ人。
1974年岩国基地に米軍海兵隊として来日、その後日本、韓国で活動。
退役後、国際基督教大学、警備会社を経て、役者として「釣りバカ日誌8」等、ナレーターとして「足立美術館音声ガイド」等、日本で活動。
現在は結婚式牧師、「日出処から」代表講師。
著書に『アメリカ人が語る アメリカが隠しておきたい日本の歴史』『アメリカ人が語る 日本人に隠しておけないアメリカの"崩壊"』（ハート出版）『太平洋戦争 アメリカに嵌められた日本』（ワック）『アメリカ白人の闇』（桜の花出版）などがある。

アメリカ人が語る日本の歴史
日本に迫る統一朝鮮(コリア)の悪夢

平成31年4月25日　第1刷発行

著　者　マックス・フォン・シュラー
発行者　日高裕明
発　行　株式会社ハート出版

〒171-0014 東京都豊島区池袋3-9-23
TEL.03(3590)6077　FAX.03(3590)6078
ハート出版ホームページ　http://www.810.co.jp

©Max von Schuler 2019 Printed in Japan
定価はカバーに表示してあります。
ISBN978-4-8024-0074-9　C0021
乱丁・落丁本はお取り替えいたします。ただし古書店で購入したものはお取り替えできません。

印刷・中央精版印刷株式会社

アメリカ人が語る
アメリカが隠しておきたい日本の歴史
マックス・フォン・シュラー 著
ISBN 978-4-8024-0028-2　本体 1500 円

アメリカ人が語る
日本人に隠しておけないアメリカの"崩壊"
マックス・フォン・シュラー 著
ISBN 978-4-8024-0041-1　本体 1500 円

元イスラエル大使が語る 神国日本
神代から大東亜戦争、現代まで貫く「日本精神」とは

エリ・コーヘン 著
ISBN 978-4-8024-0047-3　本体 1600 円

犠牲者120万人　祖国を中国に奪われたチベット人が語る
侵略に気づいていない日本人
ペマ・ギャルポ 著
ISBN 978-4-8024-0046-6　本体 1600 円

日本が危ない！　一帯一路の罠
マスコミが報道しない中国の世界戦略

宮崎正弘 著
ISBN 978-4-8024-0073-2　本体 1500 円

静かなる日本侵略
中国・韓国・北朝鮮の日本支配はここまで進んでいる

佐々木類 著
ISBN 978-4-8024-0066-4　本体 1600 円

最強兵器としての地政学
あなたも国際政治を予測できる！

藤井厳喜 著
ISBN 978-4-8024-0023-7　本体 1500 円